*William A. Wallace*

# The Great Eastern's Log

*Containing Her First Transatlantic Voyage and All Particulars of Her American Visit. By an Executive Officer*

William A. Wallace

**The Great Eastern's Log**

Containing Her First Transatlantic Voyage and All Particulars of Her American Visit. By an Executive Officer

ISBN/EAN: 9783954272662
Erscheinungsjahr: 2013
Erscheinungsort: Bremen, Deutschland

© maritimepress in Europäischer Hochschulverlag GmbH & Co. KG, Fahrenheitstr. 1, 28359 Bremen. Alle Rechte beim Verlag und bei den jeweiligen Lizenzgebern.

www.maritimepress.de | office@maritimepress.de

*Bei diesem Titel handelt es sich um den Nachdruck eines historischen, lange vergriffenen Buches. Da elektronische Druckvorlagen für diese Titel nicht existieren, musste auf alte Vorlagen zurückgegriffen werden. Hieraus zwangsläufig resultierende Qualitätsverluste bitten wir zu entschuldigen.*

THE

# GREAT EASTERN'S LOG.

CONTAINING

HER FIRST TRANSATLANTIC VOYAGE,

AND

ALL PARTICULARS OF HER AMERICAN VISIT.

BY

AN EXECUTIVE OFFICER.

LONDON:
BRADBURY & EVANS, 11, BOUVERIE STREET.
1860.

# INTRODUCTION.

BELIEVING the Great Eastern to have enlisted the sympathies of the British public generally; and I may say of the whole civilised world; I think it not out of place, on the satisfactory completion of her first voyage across the Atlantic, to publish a brief, but plain and unvarnished account of her doings; and the fact of my having had the honour of assisting in the navigation of this noble specimen of naval architecture to the shores of the New World and back to the Old Country, will, I trust, be a sufficient excuse for my presumption. Therefore, relying on the ever kind indulgence of a British public, I launch my little cockboat on the sea of public opinion, hoping due allowance will be made for one who now makes this his first attempt to breast its waves.

W. A. W.

# THE
# GREAT EASTERN'S LOG.

"Who would not brave the battle, storm, or wreck,
To move the monarch of her peopled deck?"—BYRON.

"Staunch and strong, a goodly vessel
That shall laugh at all disaster,
And with wave and whirlwind wrestle."—LONGFELLOW.

FEELING satisfied that there is scarcely an individual in Great Britain who has not heard of, or had the good fortune to witness, this stupendous monument of British industry and genius, it is needless for me to enter into details of her building and launching; but I will, with the reader's permission, accompany him on board, while she is lying snugly at her moorings off Netley Abbey, Southampton Water.

The Great Eastern was designed by Isambard Kingdom Brunel, Esq., and built by Scott Russell, Esq., the eminent ship-builder of Millwall, London.

The gentleman selected to command this noble ship, after the melancholy death of the lamented Captain Harrison, was John Vine Hall, well known as a skilful commander of first-class steamers. The eleven executive officers were also all men of considerable experience in steam navigation, several of them having been in command. It may interest the reader if I give here a brief description of their various duties.

The chief officer has charge of the upper deck, rigging, &c., and is also responsible for the general discipline of the ship, under the supervision of the commander. This officer keeps no watch. The second, third, and fourth officers have charge of the watches, assisted by six others, there being always three officers on watch at the same time, thus stationed: the senior on the bridge, one on the look-out forward, and the junior officer of the watch in charge of the steering. There is also a midshipman in each watch; and while at sea two quarter-masters and six seamen at the steering wheels.

The officer of the lower decks and holds has charge of everything below the upper deck, working of the cables, fire arrangements, cleanliness of lower decks, &c. The civil officers consist of a surgeon, one assistant-surgeon, and a dispenser; provedore, purser, three ship's clerks, and one provedore's clerk; these officers, with the exception of the surgeons, were under the supervision of Mr. Thomas Bold, the commercial manager of the ship. There is a chief engineer in each engine-room, who with eighteen assistant engineers, are under the immediate superintendence of Mr. McLennan, the chief engineer.

On Saturday the 9th of June, at 2 P.M., the ship slipped from her moorings and proceeded down channel on a trial trip, as far as the Start Point, being again made fast to her moorings at 2 P.M. on the following day.

The engines worked easily and well; the ship, under easy steam, having made an average rate of twelve and a half knots, or fourteen and a half statute miles per hour throughout. In consequence of her satisfactory performance, it was decided by the directors that the ship should leave for New York on the following Saturday, June 16th. Accordingly, on the afternoon of that day, steam was up and everything in readiness for a start; but in consequence of a strong gale blowing, accompanied with heavy rain, it was impossible to see our way out; it was therefore necessary to delay her sailing till the following morning.

Among our passengers were the Honourable Captain Carnegie, R. N., Messrs. Gooch and Barber, directors, Mrs. Gooch, Mr. Wood, the Times' correspondent, Mr. Murphy the New York pilot, two ladies, and thirty-six other gentlemen.

---

## THE OUTWARD VOYAGE.

"To the West, to the West, the land of the Free,
Where mighty Missouri rolls down to the sea."—RUSSEL.

ON *Sunday, June 17th*, 1860, at 8.30 A.M. the Great Eastern slipped from her moorings and effected a clear start, stopping outside the Needles at 10.40 A.M. to discharge Mr. Bowyer, the pilot. Light westerly winds, attended with rain up to three o'clock P.M., when the wind veered to N.W., blowing strong: 5.15, passed the Start, both engines working very satisfactorily; at 7 P.M., the fire hoses were screwed to the engine pumps, and led the whole length of the vessel, both on the upper and main decks: this is done every night. Our boats (of which the ship carries twenty-four) were all clear for lowering, the crews told off to their stations, and everything seen in readiness in the event of accident; our good ship in the mean time steaming gaily along at an average rate of twelve knots per hour; the look-out men from their different stations cheerfully proclaiming each half hour "All's well." It is a beautiful sight to look down from the prow of this huge ship at midnight's dreary hour, and watch the wondrous facility with which she cleaves her irresistible way through the waste of waters; a fountain, playing about ten feet high before her stem, is all the broken water to be seen around her; for owing to the great beauty of her lines, she cuts the waves with the ease and quietness of a knife; her motion being just sufficient to let you know that you have no dead weight beneath your feet, but a ship that

"Skims the waters like a thing of life,
And seems to dare the elements to strife."

Woe betide the unfortunate vessel that places herself in our path, for her destruction would be inevitable, without, in all probability, our ship sustaining any injury. As an active means of offence the powers of the great ship are hardly to be overrated. Armed with half-a-dozen of Armstrong's guns, which carry a trifle over five miles, she would singly be a match for any ordinary fleet. With superior speed, solidity, and range of fire, under what possible combination of circumstances can it be conceived that she would be other than victorious in any engagement? and if the talk should be of invasion, what an excellent effect would be produced by the sight of the great ship steaming up mid-channel. Another great desideratum obtained in the Great Eastern is the wondrous facility with which she answers her helm. In the words of the late Captain Harrison, "She steers like a pilot-boat."

During the night, several vessels passed, paying us the greatest respect by giving us a wide berth.

*June 18th.*—Moderate winds and cloudy. Passed one vessel this morning bound to the eastward. Noon. Latitude 49° 27' N. Long. 7° 57' W. Run 300 miles from the Needles. 2 P.M. Moderate breeze from S.E. with cloudy weather. Set all the trysails, foresail, and two fore-topsails, wind freshening with light rain, and gradually veering to the northward. At 11 P.M. blowing a fresh gale, with a considerable sea running. Ship's motion moderate, and very easy. Orders were given to "in square sails," but executing them was quite another matter; for, with over one hundred men on the yards, it was 5 A.M. the next morning before the sails were fast: they are very difficult to handle on account of their great size, also the weight of the heavy rope attached to them. All this is bad enough, but of course the weight of the sails is considerably increased when saturated with rain; hence the great difficulty experienced in furling them; but by the time a good gale or two has taken out some of the starch and the men work better together, we shall, no doubt, manage well enough.

*June* 19*th*.—Wind still blowing fresh from the northward, weather moderately fine; five trysails and one staysail set. A heavy sea now running; the easy motion of the ship may be understood, when I state, that many of the passengers passed the whole day on the lower deck playing skittles. Another proof of the extraordinary ease with which the ship rolls is the fact, that several tumblers stood the whole day and night on a polished marble table in the smoking-room, without being thrown down. "All's well!" is still the word, engines doing their work easily and steadily; and it is the general opinion that were the bottom of the ship denuded of the weeds, barnacles, &c., which cling to it, an increase in speed of at least two knots per hour would be the result. It must at the same time be understood that the ship is by no means doing her best; for, previous to leaving Southampton, a weight of 5 lbs. was taken off the safety valves of both engines; consequently, at the best of times, we are that 5 lbs. short of steam. The latitude at noon was 48° 43′ N., and the longitude 16° 14′ W. Course and distance made good, S. 83° W. 296 knots, or 345 statute miles. P.M. Wind the same. with fine weather, although still very cold; a moderate swell still rolling across the bosom of the broad Atlantic, the great ship acknowledging its presence by rolling very easily, and in a most dignified manner, or, as the sailors express it, "taking her time about it." We sighted two or three ships during the day; one an American, passed close to us, standing to the N.E., showing 1st pendant, No. 5972. The night was fine, the only sound heard to break its monotony being the "All's well!" of the look-out men; and a cheering sound it is on board a ship at sea, carrying comfort to many a timid heart.

The 20*th* dawned on us with a continuance of fine weather, and a light northerly wind. At noon our latitude was 47° 50′ N., and longitude 22° 54′ W. Distance run, S. 77 W. 284 knots, or 330 statute miles. For two hours during the morning the ship had been run on different courses, for the purpose of comparing the compasses, thus detracting from the ship's run about sixteen miles. Towards the afternoon, the wind, which had been gradually shifting, commenced freshening up from the S.S.W., with a dull, cloudy appearance; five trysails and one staysail were set to catch a little of it. A betting mania seemed to have seized the passengers to-day. Bets were made upon every conceivable thing, the number of sails that would be seen, number of knots run, of days she would be on her passage; the wind was not even spared, and many were the bets made as to whether we should have more or less, come a-head or go astern, &c.; however, at midnight, the wind itself settled the question by blowing the best part of a gale from the southward, accompanied by constant rain,—a matter of no moment to those below, but exceedingly uncomfortable for those on deck.

*Thursday, 21st.*—A miserable morning, the wind blowing fresh from the S.W., with thick rainy weather. At 10 A.M., the wind had veered more to the westward, and we were compelled to take in all sail. At noon we found ourselves in latitude 49° 16′ N., longitude 29° 57′ W., having run S. 74° W., 305 knots, or 355 statute miles, making an average of 12¾ knots per hour, a slight improvement, although the want of steam is still badly felt. The ship is labouring under every disadvantage, being some six feet by the stern, and having a very foul bottom, which, with the deficiency of steam, tends materially to decrease her speed. This evening passed away very pleasantly, a Great Eastern harmonic meeting being held in the saloon, Captain Hall adding to the amusement by playing several airs on the flute, accompanied by the cornet-à-piston and piano-forte; there was also some very tolerable singing.

"Lights out" at 11 P.M. put an end to the evening's amusements, and was a signal for all hands to bed. The heat in the paddle-engine room is very great, the thermometer standing at 110°, making it very distressing for the engineers on watch. The wind has veered to the northward, blowing fresh, with squalls, enabling us to make sail, but only for an hour or two, as it again decreased so that the sails had to be once more furled.

*Friday, 22nd.*—Strong winds (very variable and squally, from N.W. to S.W.), with thick weather and heavy rain. Before noon the wind veered to N.W., a moderate breeze and tolerably fine weather, but still cold. The crew are employed scraping upper and lower decks, and getting the ship generally as clean as time will permit. At noon our latitude was 44° 51′ N., longitude 36° 23′ W., the run S. 73° W., 284 knots or 331 statute miles. During the afternoon—which was fine, with a moderate head-wind—we passed a British barque steering as ourselves, also a ship steering S.W. The monotony of the afternoon was diversified by some animated foot-races round the deck between American and English competitors, the "Lion" gaining the victory over the "Eagle." The principal place of attraction to the passengers is the paddle-engine room skylight, where some of them stand for hours watching the revolutions of the huge machinery; but the dinner-bugle blowing, "The Roast Beef of Old England" has an attraction attached to it which soon clears the deck of all interested parties; the same interest attaches to the tea-bugle—"Polly Put the Kettle on."

*Saturday, 23rd.*—Light head-winds with thick weather and a drizzling rain—continued so up to noon. The 5lbs. pressure was restored to the safety-valves of the paddle-engines, but it was found impossible to do so with the screw-engines, the valves being adjusted from the inside of the boilers; consequently it could only be done by stopping and blowing-off, which would have taken some hours, and caused too great a detention. The consumption of coal since leaving has averaged 260 tons per day; this has, of course, lightened the ship, and given more slip to both screw and paddles, averaging about 12 per cent. At noon we were in latitude 42° 50′ N., longitude 42° 40′ W. Distance run 301 knots, 351 statute miles.

P.M. Weather still the same, and as we are now on the banks of Newfoundland, and in the latitude where ice may be expected, the thermometer was kept in constant use to test the temperature of the water, which altered in two or three hours from 68° to 53°. This being a sure sign that ice was in the vicinity, and the weather being so thick as to render a look-out useless, Captain Hall prudently determined to keep the ship more to the southward, clear of ice; and, by so doing, set the growlers at work, as by going to the southward we have to contend with a strong adverse current, thus giving up all chance of making the passage in ten days; however, "discretion is the better part of valour." The weather continued thick all night, with fresh baffling winds, squally, and very cold, with occasional rain.

*Sunday, 24th.*—Fresh northerly winds, and cloudy; four trysails, two topsails, and one staysail set; mustered the ship's company, in blue, at 10.30, A.M.; tolled the bell for church, and at 11 commenced divine service in first dining-saloon, which was performed by a clergyman-passenger. At noon we were in latitude 41° 2′ N., longitude 48° 53′ W.; run 300 knots, or 350 statute miles. This, being Sunday, was kept in a manner suitable to the day, the passengers lounging listlessly about the deck, gazing at the working of the machinery, watching the ship's progress through the water, or reading. No irrelevant amusement was indulged in, not even a bet being made, but one and all seemed to be impressed with a wish to "remember the Sabbath day, and keep it holy."

Exchanged colours with an American schooner; also a ship standing to the eastward. Toward midnight the wind decreased, and came right a-head. Furled all sails.

*Monday, 25th.*—A dead calm, the sun rising over a sea resembling glass; the heavens without a cloud, and the heat, as the sun approached its altitude, such as might be expected in the tropics. We are now evidently in the gulf-stream, contesting with its (to us) adverse current of about two miles per hour. Quantities of the yellow gulf-weed, covered with small leaves of the same colour, floating on the surface of the water, gives ample testimony of our whereabouts. Passed several vessels becalmed; had some considerable trouble with one of our seamen—a big powerful fellow, an advocate for the use of the knife: placed him in irons, and secured him below, with the intention of discharging him at New York. It is worthy of remark, that there has been a total absence among the passengers of that terrible nausea—sea-sickness; for, during the whole passage, we have not heard of one case, even among the ladies; another proof of the steadiness with which our good ship "rules the waves." Our latitude, at noon, was 40° 48' N., longitude 56° 10' W., and distance run 325 knots, or 379 statute miles. At 4 P.M. a light wind sprung up from the S.E., enabling us to set a little canvas to woo its favours. A slight alarm was caused by some of the coals in one of the bunkers becoming heated, and, as was supposed, in danger of ignition. Numerous fire-hoses (always ready) were immediately brought into requisition, but happily were not needed, it being a false alarm.

*Tuesday, 26th.*—The wind this morning was the same as yesterday, but a thick haze covered the water, rendering it difficult to see any distance a-head of the ship. At noon our latitude was 40° 58' N., longitude 63° 31.' W., distance run 335 knots, or 391 statute miles; an average of 14 knots per hour. Passed two vessels, and at 3 P.M. became suddenly enveloped in a thick fog, so thick that no pair of eyes could penetrate further than twenty feet from the vessel. The steam-whistles were all set going as per Admiralty regulations, and such a yelling and screeching as they made surely never was heard; loud and deep were the curses bestowed on them, and many were the fingers thrust into ears to keep out a portion of the unearthly row; but it was no use, the fog would continue, steam-whistles would scream, so there was nothing for it but to grin and bear it with Christian fortitude. As night approached it became evident to our ever-careful commander, that, for the sake of humanity, speed must be slackened, for collision with any vessel, at our then rate of speed, would have been for her instant destruction; so, with his usual promptitude, he gave orders for "half speed" on both screw and paddles. Although fully convinced of its necessity, we were all sorry when the order was given, for we had made up our minds that a great run would have been the result of this day's work.

Towards midnight, at the request of Mr. Murphy, our New York pilot, the engines, for the first time, were stopped, and an attempt made to find bottom with 120 fathoms of line, but without success. After half-an-hour's detention we again proceeded leisurely on our course: the fog continuing the whole of the night.

*Wednesday, 27th.*—The fog had cleared up a little, and at 5 A.M. we again stopped and obtained soundings in sixty-five fathoms on St. George's Bank, then proceeding at full speed for our destination. At 10 A.M. the fog had nearly disappeared, the sun again making its appearance; at 11 A.M. ran close by a New York pilot-schooner, they saluted us by dipping their colours and firing a gun. Notwithstanding all our stoppages, going half-speed, &c., we had, up to noon, run the distance of 254 knots or 305 miles, our distance from Sandy Hook being 234 knots or 371 miles. The ship being some seven feet by the stern, it was deemed advisable, before attempting to cross the bar at New York, to bring her, if possible, nearer to an even keel; accordingly about 800 tons of water were pumped into the fore compartment, which made a slight improvement in her trim. The night was fine, but a thick haze settled over the horizon where the land should have been seen, preventing us catching a glimpse of the coast lights.

*Thursday, 28th.*—At 4 A.M. stopped and sounded in twenty-one fathoms, proving that we were in the vicinity of the Sandy Hook light-ship, so the engines were kept going quite slowly. As far as distance is concerned, this virtually finishes the voyage; and taking stoppages into consideration it has been performed in ten-and-a-half days; but we feel satisfied that under more favourable circumstances three days may be deducted from this time. At 6.20 A.M., the Navesink Highlands were barely discernible through the haze. At 7.20 passed the Sandy Hook light-vessel (receiving a salute of two guns from her), and stopped the engines, having to wait till 2.30 P.M., for high water on the bar. A lottery which had been got up during the voyage, by fifty members, at 10s. each, for the time the light-ship should be passed, was won by two of our officers. During the morning, the following address, drawn up and signed by all the passengers, was presented to Captain Hall—

"To Captain John Vine Hall.

"Great Eastern, June 17, 1860.

"Dear Sir,—We, the undersigned passengers, who have the honour of being the first to cross the Atlantic in your magnificent vessel, cannot now, at the conclusion of our pleasant voyage, separate without expressing our opinion of the great merits of this triumph of engineering skill and naval architecture.

"Our voyage, though fine, has yet (as is generally the case in Atlantic passages) been sufficiently checkered with rough weather to demonstrate that, in point of seaworthiness, the Great Eastern has no equal in the world. We are aware that the incredulity and prejudice which oppose all great undertakings when first attempted have been manifested to an almost unusual extent against this noble vessel. On no point has this feeling been more strongly shown than with regard to her manageability at sea.

"Her conduct during the brief storm of the 18th and 19th inst., should put all such fears (if any still exist after this voyage) at rest for ever.

"Her movements, even when the gale was strongest, were slow and easy, and at all times so much less than those of the best sea-going steamers as to be quite removed from any standard of comparison. Those who know by experience what an Atlantic passage really is, will appreciate the high praise bestowed when we express our belief that the Great Eastern, in accommodation, safety, and freedom from disturbing motion, is as much superior to ordinary vessels as she surpasses them in magnitude and power.

"The supposed necessity of working her engines at a low rate of speed for some days has prevented her effecting that rapid passage which we are convinced she can easily accomplish. Yet, from what we have seen, we express our firm belief that the Great Eastern, in proper trim, is capable of making greater speed than has yet been attained at sea. Such a result will be due not more to her unequalled form than to the efficiency and power of her engines. That the latter will always be found equal to their duty is witnessed by the fact that during the whole of our run from Southampton to New York they have worked with the utmost ease and steadiness, never requiring even a moment's stoppage for attention or adjustment of anything. We fully appreciate the anxious vigilance which has been exercised by yourself and your officers in all relating to the safety of the ship and the general comfort of the passengers.

"In taking leave of you we most heartily wish every success to yourself and the noble vessel which you have the distinguished honour to command, and remain, &c."

Then follow the signatures of all the passengers.

The answer of Captain Hall was as follows:—

"To the Chairman of Meeting of Passengers.

"Great Eastern, off Sandy Hook, June 28, 1860.

"Dear Sir,—I am very highly gratified with the comprehensive and expressive address which you have just presented to me from the passengers. I value it the more as it so simply, yet justly, points out the peculiar excellencies of the Great Eastern, being at the same time free from undue panegyric, and stating only facts, and opinions based upon those facts. The expression of satisfaction at the endeavour of my officers and self to promote the comfort and safety of the ship is, and will continue to be, highly appreciated by us. In return, we beg to thank you, on behalf of the passengers, for the unvarying courtesy we have received from them, and only regret that our acquaintance should be so short. With the best wishes for the happiness and prosperity of every one among the present passengers—the select few who were the first to have practical faith in the great ship,

"I remain, dear Sir, with much esteem, yours faithfully,
"JOHN VINE HALL."

For the first hour or so after stopping our engines, we lay pretty quiet, surrounded by vessels becalmed in what appeared a sea of oil, so smooth and motionless was it, whilst the piercing rays of the sun pouring down upon our heads, rendered absolutely necessary the order, "Hands, spread awnings;" but this monotony was soon broken, first by the arrival of the steam tug "Yankee," chartered by our New York agents, Messrs. Grinnell and Minturn, having on board the secretary to the Big-ship Company, Mr. Yates, and about 150 representatives of the press, and friends. This party were (with but few exceptions) the only persons admitted on board during the day. After the arrival of the "Yankee," steamers of all size and build, crammed with passengers from their upper story (for the American river steamers have all a one or two-story house above the deck) to their guard-rails, swarmed around us, the crowds on board filling the air with their cheers,—three being given for everything in any way connected with the Great Eastern,—waving their hats and handkerchiefs with might and main; the firing of guns, playing of bands, blowing of steam whistles, and the indescribable row made by so large an assembly of live Yankees, being quite deafening and bewildering. A light breeze now springing up, yachts and vessels of every size and rig were added to the strength of our escort; but as a description of our reception will come better from an American pen, we will leave our friend, Mr. Osbon, of the "New York World," to report our arrival and reception.

"At twenty minutes past seven o'clock the Great Eastern arrived off the light-ship. She was received by Captain Cosgrove, with a salute and the dipping of colours.

"Immediately the news of her arrival was telegraphed to the consignees of the ship, Messrs. Grinnell, Minturn & Co. The sails were refurled, the yards squared, and the ship put in order to come up to the city when the tide should serve, which would be between two and three o'clock in the afternoon. The anchors were cockbilled, and the cables put in readiness to anchor, if necessary; but owing to the smoothness of the sea, it was not deemed advisable to anchor, and as the ship was under such complete control of the engines and helm. She was boarded by Mr. John Hall, news collector of the associated press, and Mr. John Van Dusen, Mr. Murphy's partner, of the pilot boat Washington, No. 4.

"The vessels which were inward bound, as they saw the huge hull, were at no loss to know it was the Great Eastern, and they hoisted their flags, and sailed close to her, and scrutinised her through their spy glasses, and in some instances sailed around her to have a good survey of the great sea monster; the crews were scattered up aloft, out on the yards, and were intently engaged in gazing upon her; the pilot boats skimmed around her, and all the vessels dipped their colours; numbers of yachts which were anchored in shore, got under weigh and spread their canvas to the light breeze and stood out to greet her. The scene was one of the liveliest interest; as far as the eye could reach up the bay, vessels were getting under way to come down. From the time of her arrival off the light-ship until she started for the bar nothing occurred of interest, except that the consignees and the representatives of the press came down in the steamer Yankee and boarded the ship. Several other boats came down, but no one was allowed on board, until the Health Officer should board her.

"As soon as it was light enough to see anything, the people of Staten Island began to pour out of their houses, the earliest risers taking care to secure positions commanding the most extensive view. In their eagerness to catch the first glimpse of the approaching steamer, as well as to retain their places, breakfast was forgotten, personal discomforts were overlooked, and nought was thought of but the Great Eastern. The hours crept on apace till the watches told eight o'clock, and their patience was still unrewarded. Quarter-past eight came, but with no encouragement to the gazing multitudes. Five minutes more, and a voice cried out, "I see her!" and immediately it passed from man to man that the looked-for steamer was in sight. Instinctively the noise was hushed, each one held his breath, stretched to his utmost height, and strained his eyes to get a sight of the mighty stranger. But it was only the possessors of spy-glasses who were the fortunate ones. A few minutes more and the Great Eastern came within the range of vision of the most short-sighted. Then it was the pent-up enthusiasm burst forth, and one long shout told of the joy which was felt at the success of the great enterprise. Recovering from this, the boatmen hastened to their crafts, and in less time than it takes us to describe their efforts, countless little sail-boats were on their way out to sea. Quickly the news spread along the island, and soon the eastern side was lined with spectators.

"Meanwhile the people in the city were by no means idle. The telegram to Messrs. Grinnell, Minturn & Co., served as a signal for all the 'packet steamboats' to fire up and start down the bay. Passengers were only too glad to embark, despite the charge of one dollar a head that was levied by the proprietors of these boats. As fast as one boat was filled another came up, and before noon the Thomas Hunt, Owen Petitt, W. G. Putnam, Delaware, and many others, were shooting down the bay in search of the Great Eastern. The yachts, too, that were lying quietly at anchor, soon displayed signs of life; the sails were run up, the flags hoisted, and they joined the fleet of steamboats that were hastening seaward. As time and tide wait for no man, the spectators had to wait for the tide, for the huge steamer refused to gratify the waiting multitudes until it was high water.

"At a quarter of eleven o'clock yesterday morning, a small steamer, with the appropriate cognomen, 'Yankee,' was hastily procured and hired by the consignees of the big ship, Messrs. Grinnell and Minturn, and still more hastily boarded by the representatives of the press, who had previously mustered in goodly numbers at Messrs. Grinnell and Minturn's office, and as soon as the Yankee came alongside of the wharf at the foot of Maiden Lane, they jumped aboard like so many literary pirates, as it were, determined to slaughter their mammoth prize by piecemeal, and do her up in detail. All the enterprise and ingenuity of reportorial talent were present, from sentiment down to burlesque; matter of fact and statistics; political, law, and Wall-street lore; satire and argument; everything in the way of newspaper talent that appears in black and white, and in close columns was freighted on the Yankee. The shipping moored to the wharves in the vicinity of the steam-tug, and the moving craft of steam and sail, of all descriptions, seemed to be perfectly unconscious of the nearness of their expected, august visitor. Not a flag was waving, excepting the scanty pieces of bunting long worn there by the winds of many a clime, nor a gun booming as the sombre little vessel steamed quietly through the bay and out beyond the Narrows on her course to the 'John Bull' of naval architecture. The fort on Governor's Island and Fort Hamilton with its opposite neighbour, were bathing in the sunlight, and seemed to be in an undisturbed stony sleep; the picturesque shores of Staten Island dotted with cottages and covered with the greenest of foliage, the long, strongly marked white beach line of Long Island, were rapidly passed as the little Yankee slyly glided into the open sea to meet the great vessel.

"The whole trip was pleasant and unmarked by anything unusual; members of the press always have a press in their heads, a press on their thoughts, and a press on their words and actions; in fact, they are compressed, and, as usual, on this occasion they all looked as little ruffled, as quiet and subdued as the placid bay on which they were sailing.

"As the little steamer was flitting like a butterfly around a buffalo, the band on board the Eastern struck up the national air, 'Hail Columbia.' After taking one tour of inspection, she neared the big hull, and, having been lashed to a tug which had been previously moored to the Eastern, the consignees and representatives of the press stepped aboard. But here a difficulty occurred: the adjoining tug was not sufficiently near the side of the big ship to allow the passengers to step from her deck to the gangway ladders, the bottom step of which was higher than the deck of the Yankee. A plank, however, with some difficulty, was soon adjusted, and the gentlemen stepped, one by one, from the tug on to the gangway ladders, and all reached the lofty deck without a drenching in the waves, or injury to any one.

"When stepping upon the deck for the first time, one is slightly disappointed, after witnessing the graceful curves and the beautiful proportions of her exterior, to see the apparently worn and old look of the decks and companion ways. This is undoubtedly owing to the hasty departure of the Great Eastern, and to the previous doubt and suspension as to her final destination. The consignees were immediately greeted by Captain John Vine Hall, and several members of the press by the other officers; the crowd, however, soon dispersed, and was soon no longer a crowd.

"Immediately after the formality of greeting was over, the consignees and the other guests descended to the second cabin on a tour of inspection. There, in an adjoining room, the passengers were found at dinner. They seemed to be startled by the appearance of so many visitors. A brass band at the same time was discoursing some lively strains.

"In the meanwhile the remainder of the visitors had scattered themselves in all directions over the wide expanse of deck, some were at the bow looking down at her stern, others in the raised grating of the quarterdeck, examining the wheels that guide the rudder and trying to catch a glimpse of the fans of the screw, sixty feet below; others were peering into the wheel-boxes, where the immense red frame work was lit up, when they were in motion, by a beautiful rainbow; certainly an odd, though not unusual sight—a rainbow within the wheel of a steamship. And others were gazing down into the abyss of the paddle engine machinery, where the stupendous oscillating engines were in motion. Indeed, this sight was truly grand. The precision of the motion of such an immense mass, at such a depth; the groaning of the steam, as it were, in the bowels of the monster, and the ease of motion of each stupendous piston, were calculated to inspire emotions of awe and wonder.

" The lively scene on the deck was rendered more pleasing by the bright buttoned uniforms of the courteous officers, who paced to and fro, cheerfully explaining everything, and readily imparting all kinds of nautical information.

" It is strange, however it should have happened, that such a scene was not graced by those who are always present, where manhood is triumphant, and intellect and skill are victorious over matter. We noticed but one lady on board, the wife of one of the directors.

" Before the giant of steam marine had made a revolution of her paddles for the start to the city, a number of little craft had reached her, crowded down to the water's edge, and white with handkerchiefs, waved by eager spectators, who sent up cheer after cheer most heartily, for the great triumph of naval architecture. The O. M. Petit, the Thomas Hunt, and a little black, walnut-shaped steamer, sailed in this jubilant manner, round and round, like timid Lilliputians, reconnoitering an awe-inspiring Brobdingnag.

" At fifteen minutes past two o'clock the signal was given and the engines were put in motion. Slowly the immense paddle-wheels revolved, and the vast ship was quickly under way. Those who had not seen her in motion, were astonished at the ease, quietness and perfect grace of her movements. From the steamboats and vessels surrounding her, were sent up deafening cheers of cordial approval, while the ladies, who made up one-half of the visiting steamboat loads, waved their handkerchiefs in ecstacies of delight. The enthusiasm was great—the scene was exciting.

" On board the immense steamer every man knew his place, and with the certainty and regularity of clockwork, all her movements were guided. There was perfect harmony of action, perfect control. Her broad wakes—for she had to make quite a circuit in getting started—looked from the stern of the steamer as a vast river winding through a boundless prairie looks to the æronaut. Compared with it, the wakes of the smaller vessels following in her track sank into narrow nothingness.

"A few minutes' time brought the huge steamer near the bar. Now came the trying time. The great problem was to be solved, whether she could cross the bar. Every one watched with eagerness her approach. On the result depended whether the steamer could enter the harbour of New York. She was drawing 26 feet 6 inches of water, and the tide favoured her with 29 feet. The wind is light; everything is propitious. The bar is reached. The huge form of the steamer goes over. There is no sensation of grounding. Without touching ground the bar is crossed. The Great Eastern is in the harbour of New York. It is a proud victory. Anxiety is at an end. A salute of twenty guns heralds the victory. Shrill whistles from the accompanying fleet of steamers, ringing of bells and cheers of thousands of spectators, who have been waiting and watching with nervous anxiety the result, attest appreciation of the steamer's triumph.

"Promise of a dinner on board the mammoth steam-ship was made on the little steam-tug Yankee. The ride down the bay and the sea air had sharpened the appetite. In the excitement of wandering about the huge vessel, marching up and down her immense decks, looking into the complex wilderness of rooms below, and observing the vast engines and towering display of masts, the keen hunger of which nearly everybody had been complaining, was forgotten. At half-past two o'clock, however, when an invitation to dinner was extended to the new comers on board, a general and hearty response to the same was manifested by a rush to the dining-room. The tables were set in the second dining saloon. A sumptuous repast covered them—the leading staple articles being solid English roast beef and Southdown mutton. Champagne goblets and ice formed the accompaniments, with a bounteous supply of bottled English ale. All ate and drank with a relish.

"Now that the trying rubicon has been passed, the remainder of the trip to the city is straightforward. But there is excitement and intense enthusiasm all the way, such as never before attended the arrival of any vessel in New York. The day was one of the most delightful imaginable. A delicious breeze came from the south-west, and the sky was cloudless, affording a splendid view of the bay, and Staten Island, and Long Island shores. From the deck of the Great Eastern, the view of the outstretching harbour of New York was unparalleled in extent and beauty. Strangers on board the vessel, who for the first time were entering the harbour of New York, were overwhelmed with wonder at the splendid scene revealing itself to their astonished gaze. Old residents of the city looked on with equal wonderment.

"As the Great Eastern neared New York, the fleet of vessels, crowded with people anxious to see the monster leviathan of the commercial world, increased in numbers. There was a proportionate increase of enthusiasm, and wild fluttering of flags, and gratulatory salutes and ringing of bells. Yachts and sailing vessels crowded in among the nautical visitants. As each came within hailing distance, the sailors swung their hats, and the ladies described jubilant circles in the air with their handkerchiefs. To the salutes, appropriate and hearty responses were made from the steamer.

"From Fort Hamilton a national salute was fired, which was responded to by the booming of cannon from the decks of the Great Eastern.

"The report on the bulletin board of the newspapers, that the tide would be high enough at half-past one o'clock to float the Great Eastern over the bar, induced many thousands of people to assemble on the battery at that time to witness the giant steamship as she passed up the bay. It was not understood, however, that the great vessel was anchored off the Lightship some forty miles from the city, and that the actual passage of the dangerous bar could only take place between three and four o'clock. Very many, after remaining in the broiling sun over two hours, and straining their eyes until they ached, left for home, and voted the monster vessel a humbug. However, at five o'clock, about which time she hove in sight, there was a vast crowd on the Battery, and all the neighbouring wharves were densely thronged. Telescopes, opera and magnifying glasses, of all kinds, were brought into requisition, most of which, it was evident, were more ornamental than useful, and obscured rather than helped the sight. A fine view of the Great Eastern was obtained from the balcony of Castle Garden, to which a favoured few were admitted.

"The first sign of the Great Eastern which greeted the anxious watchers on the Battery was a dense cloud of smoke, which made its appearance over Long Island; and shortly after, her tall masts loomed up over the point which juts into the lower bay. Presently the huge hulk hove in sight, and soon darkened all of the horizon that can be seen between the Staten and Long Island coasts. The guns flashed out a thunderous welcome, flags were hoisted and dipped, and myriads of sail and row boats dashed out into the bay to surround, survey, and cheer the great vessel.

"After passing the Narrows, the Great Eastern 'hugged' the Staten Island shore; and at this time, owing to the distance, and the darkened background, she did not look as large as people were led to expect, and there was some disappointment in consequence. It was not until she approached the Battery that her vast proportions became manifest; but the best test of her enormous bulk was the dwarfing of every large vessel she neared or passed. The steam-ship Niagara, which was lying in the stream, bedecked with flags and steamers, shrunk apparently to the dimensions of a little ferry boat, and a good-sized revenue cutter seemed scarcely above her water-line, and one would suppose could hardly survive a ripple from her bow. As the great vessel passed the Battery, salutes were fired by the Asia from her dock at Jersey City, by the Niagara and the revenue cutter, and all the vessels dipped their flags as she passed. The beauty of the day, the myriads of boats on the river, the shipping in the offing gaily adorned with flags and streamers, and, towering above them all, the great nautical wonder of the age, was a scene not often witnessed nor soon forgotten.

"Long before the time at which she was announced by the papers as likely to arrive, the Great Eastern was the principal subject of conversation along the North River. Everybody communicated what little he knew about her to everybody else; and the large amount of information of which some inveterate talkers were possessed was very marvellous, considering that none of it was correct. The chairs were brought out from all the drinking-houses to the side-walk, and were occupied by the waiting multitude. Some there were of patient individuals, who sat for two or three hours on the docks, in the hot sun, agonising and perspiring, waiting and longing for her approach, determined to see her, if she came at all. We presume they had a fine time of it. Perhaps, however, they were right in thinking that to see the vessel pursuing her course up the harbour, was a hundred times better than to see her lying quietly and motionless at the dock. It may be very interesting to look upon the skeleton of a mastodon, but the grand sight would be to behold the great animal moving in his native forests.

"By three o'clock the ends of all the piers along the way were covered with people. The top of a pile of timbers was sure to be occupied by a crowd. The docks near Hammond Street were covered by large numbers of people. An occasional sailor in the masts of a ship stood ready to give the signal of the approach of the vessel. A cry, in joke, of 'Here she comes!' would make the ropes alive with boys. The men speculated on the time she would arrive, and the little boys pointed out the masts of vessels almost out of sight, very positive that all belonged to the Great Eastern. One little fellow thought that if he could go up in a balloon he could tell just where she was. The firing of cannon was the signal for increased vigilance on the part of lookers-out, and in a short time after this the vessel came in sight. When she came near enough to be fully observed, the admiration, astonishment, and enthusiasm were unbounded. The men cheered involuntarily, the boys uttered prolonged enunciations of the syllable 'oh!' and every person commenced to point out to his neighbour some peculiar or wonderful thing which he observed about her. The masts of the ships were now covered with human beings, numerous as fruit on an apple-tree. Old gentlemen, seized with unwonted vitality, essayed to climb the rope-ladders, and sailors shouted to 'land-lubbers,' in derision, to look out and not fall. The roofs of houses that were near enough to afford a view of the river were covered with ladies and children, as well as men. As the vessel approached Hammond Street the crowd increased, until there seemed to be no end to it. The universal emotion was admiration and astonishment. Some, indeed, from benighted neighbourhoods, who had been told by erudite friends that she was about seven miles long, and that a livery stable was in successful operation on board of her, on account of the pleasure the passengers derived from taking morning rides of fourteen miles or so, from stem to stern and back again, and who had implicitly believed all the comic papers had said about her, were perhaps somewhat disappointed at finding her only a quarter of a mile in length, but were constrained to admit that she was a 'great baste.'

"At Hammond Street she was a long time manœuvring in the river, seeming to be attempting to turn about, but without success. She ran very near to the Jersey City shore, and lay there for a considerable time; then she bore down directly towards the pier at the foot of Hammond Street, and every one supposed that she was coming in. Changing her course, however, she started up the stream, and went so far as to be out of sight from that locality.

"As the vessel steamed up the river, the spectacle presented was not a whit inferior to that along the harbour. The gaily decorated boats that shot hither and thither across the stream, the flags flying from every mast-head, and, not the least, the huzzaing multitudes on either shore, made a *coup d'œil* that has never been surpassed since the arrival of the Great Britain fifteen years ago. The ship steamed steadily on, only to meet with new sights at every turn of the wheels, to be greeted with additional cannon salutes and shouts of welcome from the throngs crowding the encompassing steamers and vessels, and the shores.

"Nothing of importance occurred last night at the moorings of the Great Eastern. During the earlier part of the evening a large crowd, of which nearly one-half was composed of ladies, was continually on the dock, and the streets leading to the place were thronged with persons going to or returning from the place of attraction. After ten o'clock but few persons remained, except uncivilised boys and men used to sitting up late at night. During all the evening the scene was quiet and picturesque. The great vessel stood by the dock like a mighty cloud, and those on the pier gazed up in wonder, and almost in awe, at the magnificent work of human hands before them. The moon shone bright and clear upon the river, and the calm waters glistened and sparkled in its light.

"There was no other illumination of the scene than this. Darkness was spread over the great city like a black mantle, and the flickering of lamps here and there only served to make the darkness more palpable. The bulwarks seemed as high as the roof of a four-story house. Standing at one end, the other was dim and indistinctly defined in the distance. Occasionally, a boat paddled between the ship and the wharf, only noticed by the noise of the oars and the white garments of the rowers. Some of the crew of the Great Eastern leaned over the side above, and quietly gazed out upon the river and the city, or, when the crowd below grew noisy, answered questions which were asked them. The crowd below stood either on the docks or on the piles of boards, from ten to fifteen feet high, close beside the ship. Late in the evening the governing classes came out strong, and had much to say to the crew.

"One young gentleman gave utterance to the information that the crowd thought of giving the ship a white-washing that night; and another was anxious to know how the weather was up there. With the exception of these harmless passages between those who had no eye to beauty or sublimity, the quiet and want of excitement was remarkable. During the latter part of the evening, several of the seamen of the Great Eastern, with great agility, slid down a rope at the side of the vessel to the dock. The police, discovering this, loosened the rope, and ordered the sailors on board to haul it up. 'Oh, no,' they replied, 'I can't; I haven't got the heart.' The rope was then fastened by the sailors, so that it was as available as a means of escape from the ship as before. The police, baffled at this, muttered that they would lock up the next man that came down, and considered it useless to attempt anything more. And thus the monarch of the waters lay last night in the calm moonlight, waiting for the excitement of this morning. The interior of the vessel will probably be exhibited soon, if not to-day, at a stated price of admission."

*Friday, June 29th.*—Our crew, assisted by a number of shore hands, are employed cleaning ship and preparing generally for the reception of visitors. The officers of the ship to-day received a letter from the proprietors of the Astor-house hotel, offering to us all the hospitalities of their house : we were all much impressed with, and in suitable terms acknowledged, the kindness of their offer, but preferred maintaining our independence. The scene this day alongside the ship presented a most animated appearance, thousands of people gazing at the " big ship " from " early morn " to " dewy eve." Itinerant vendors of stores of all kinds ; " iced lemonade" made from lemons " grown on board the big ship," one cent per glass. " Great Eastern drinks," " cakes," " sweetmeats," and everything to which they could apply the name of the ship, commanded a ready sale. The spare ground on the wharf is letting in lots at fabulous prices for the erection of " lager bier" saloons and refreshment booths of all kinds ; there is also in course of construction a tent for the Great French Giant, M. Joseph Adams, Menagerie of Bears, Shooting Galleries, &c. &c. ; in short, the heterogeneous collection of a country fair is being fast gathered together. The Japanese (who leave in a day or two) are quite forgotten, or, rather eclipsed, by the arrival of the big ship—one set of " Great Easterns " driven out by the arrival of another " Great Eastern "—our American cousins seeming determined to apply to us the motto " Palmam qui meruit ferat." This evening two of our stokers unfortunately met their death while in a state of intoxication ; one falling from the wheel sustained concussion of the brain and died the next day ; the other fell overboard and was drowned, his body not being recovered. The ship has hitherto been a temperance one, no spirits being allowed, but now the crew have facilities for obtaining the much-coveted drink, they seem determined to make up for their long abstinence. Drunkenness is doubtless the curse of British seamen, and a frightful per-centage of death and disease is the result of this dreadful infatuation. The next day a coroner's inquest was held on board on the body of the man who was killed, a verdict of " accidental death" being returned : he is to be buried to-morrow. At the request of the proprietors of the New York Illustrated News, the whole of the officers sat for their photographs at the establishment of Mr. Gurney, Broadway, for insertion in the next week's paper. Two large and commodious gangways for " entrance " and " exit," a ticket office, &c., have been constructed, and turnstiles fixed in the interior of the ship. The general arrangement for admitting the public will be completed on Monday, and the ship thrown open on Tuesday at a charge of one dollar per head, half price to juveniles. We are blessed with beautiful weather, although it is rather too warm to be comfortable. To render the position of the ship a safe one in the event of a blow, seven anchors are buried on different parts of the wharf, and attached to these are large chains secured on board. Small steamers are constantly hovering round the ship crowded with people, who are induced to take an outside view by the flaming announcement that the fare is only 10 cents (= to 5*d*.). Nearly every steamer passing, that is possessed with anything in the shape of a band, compliments us by striking up with all the vigour of sound lungs, " God save the Queen," finishing up with three cheers for the Great Eastern.

The following is the advertisement of the directors fixing the day for opening, and the price of admission :—

" Notice is hereby given, that the Great Eastern will be prepared for the reception of visitors on Tuesday 3rd July, between the hours of nine in the morning and six in the evening. The price of admission is fixed at one dollar each for adults, and fifty cents for children under twelve years of age. By order of the directors. J. H. YATES, Secretary."

*Sunday, July* 1*st*, was fine but very warm, the dust from the shore blowing over the ship in clouds, adding much to our discomfort. At 10 A.M. the clergyman who was to officiate at the interment of the fireman who was killed on Friday last, attended, and the crew being assembled on the quarter deck, he spoke a few earnest words to them on the evils attending drunkenness, as exemplified in the untimely end of their two shipmates, exhorting them in the most solemn terms to reform their ways ; the coffin was then lowered over the side enveloped in the shroud of a British sailor—the flag he loves so well in life, that covers him at death—the Union Jack. The ship's bells were tolled, and about 120 men from the engineers' department, headed by their chief, and accompanied by some ten or twelve other engineers, formed a procession following the hearse which carried the body to the grave ; it was a mournful sight, and one that should have been a lesson to them ; but no, the same night in a drunken row one man had his head split open by his messmate with a bar of iron, his death being at first feared. The dastardly coward, who committed the assault, was sent to gaol, and was sentenced to undergo a lengthened period of imprisonment, so that we were well quit of him. I should think on a moderate computation, no less than 50,000 persons have embraced the opportunity presented by an idle day to have a look at the Great Eastern from the wharf; and what with tents, stalls, &c., the display of flags, the cries of the intinerant vendors of all sorts, and the immense motley multitude swarming on the wharf attired in all the colours of the rainbow, I was forcibly reminded of Greenwich fair as it used to be. The weather on the succeeding day, Monday, was all that heart could desire. Painters were making a vain attempt to beautify the exterior of the ship, but no sooner was the paint laid on than it was covered with a shower of dust, making all colours alike. Our preparations for opening the ship are now nearly completed, and she certainly looks in first-rate order.

Received a visit from Mr. Jacobs (the Wizard), and his brother (the Goblin Sprightly). We paid a visit to the theatre in which they were performing in the evening, and were much amused by their excellent entertainment. Among Mr. Jacob's friends was one " old English Gentleman," whom we had invited to view the Great Eastern by moonlight; never shall I forget his ecstasy when he stood upon her spacious quarter deck; but after ascending to the top of the paddle-box, " hold my hat and stick," said he, to one of us, and down he plumped on his knees, his white hair glistening in the moonlight, and with hands clasped, he exclaimed, " This is the proudest moment of my long life! God, I thank Thee I'm an Englishman!"

*Tuesday, July 3rd.*—At 8 A.M. the Great Eastern was first opened for admission to an American public, but contrary to our expectations there was anything but a rush, 1700 being the small number of visitors registered for the day by the turnstiles; thus showing pretty clearly that the rate of admission is too high. The general opinion of the visitors seems to be, that she's " a mighty big ship," and must have cost a " tarnation sight of dollars." The following day, being the anniversary of American Independence, was kept as a holiday throughout the entire country by all classes; " everybody " seemed bound to go " somewhere;" excursion steamers were running in all directions with " fishing parties," " picnic parties," and " parties " of all kinds; the theatres and all places of amusement held out inducements in the shape of extra bills of fare, headed with the announcement that it was the " Glorious Fourth." The greatest license appeared to be allowed to all parties. Do as you like, appeared to be the order of the day. Pistols were popping and big guns banging the whole day long, twenty-one of the latter being fired by us as a compliment to the Yankees; and in the evening the public thoroughfares were almost impassable, for squibs, crackers, and other fireworks were thrown about in a most reckless manner, many fires being the consequence. A public display of fireworks was gratuitously provided at several places; among others, at the City Hall; and being informed these would be the best, we, escorted by Mr. Rawlings, of the " New York Illustrated News," wended our way, though not without some difficulty, through the streets to the office of the " New York Times," from the upper windows of which establishment we had a good view of the display, which, in comparison with the same sort of thing we are in the habit of seeing in Old England, was, we think, rather insignificant. After the finale (which was a large scroll in coloured lights, bearing the words "American Independence," with Washington and the Goddess of Liberty, in life-like figures, steamers with their wheels turning, and sailing ships representing Commerce, finishing with a grand discharge of rockets, roman candles, &c.) we took a look into Florence's Theatre, and saw a ridiculous burlesque on the Japanese. After which, and a "claret punch" at Taylor's, (the most magnificent restaurant in New York), we returned to the ship just as the fun in the shape of fighting, &c., was commencing, but not having a taste for that style of amusement, we betook ourselves to bed. The weather next day was squally, with a considerable fall of rain; the visitors both yesterday and to-day not averaging over 1700, or 3400 for the two days. During the night we found the water-thieves very troublesome, and we have been compelled to use pistols on them once or twice, sinking some of their boats to teach them manners. On the evening of Friday the 6th, all the officers, with the exception of three, likewise the senior engineers, attended a grand banquet given in our honour, by the proprietor of the "New York Illustrated News," at "Lafarge House," one of the principal hotels in New York.

To the excellency of the entertainment, and the very kind and flattering reception given to our worthy commander and his officers, we would wish to bear testimony; the gentlemen connected with the paper being unremitting in their kind attention. We all spent a most happy evening, and shall ever think of it with pleasure.

*Saturday, July 11th.*—Fine weather, but very warm. This is the last day on which a dollar will be charged for admission. On Monday next, the ship will be open for inspection at half that amount. During the five days of the charge of a dollar, the number of visitors registered was only 8578; but the reduction of the price of admission will doubtless treble that number during the ensuing week. The directors, assisted by an experienced public caterer, Mr. Jarrett, are arranging excursion trains and steamers from different parts of the States, and every facility will be afforded to intending visitors. The next day being Sunday, the ship was closed to the public; but that the excitement caused by the arrival has in no ways abated, the following extract from one of the local papers published the following morning will prove.

"THE GREAT EASTERN.

"The principal feature of attraction in the metropolis yesterday was the Great Eastern; and never in the history of Gotham has the vicinity of Hammond, Bank, and Bethune Streets been the focus of a greater throng than was all day gathered to gratify the public curiosity. The influx commenced at an early hour in the morning, and from that time until night let down her curtain, increased by thousands. Central Park was comparatively deserted, the Sixth, Fourth, and Third avenue cars hardly doing a week-day's business, while the Eighth and Ninth Avenue cars, which run in the vicinity of the great show, were crowded to suffocation. Every street running towards the North river in the locality of the ship was black with people—men, women, and children—wending their way towards the dock. From the east side especially the delegation was immense, while those living in Williamsburg, Brooklyn, Jersey City, Hoboken, and other suburbs, had facilities provided for their accommodation in the shape of steamers and ferry-boats, which ran at frequent intervals during the day, conveying passengers around the ship at a price varying from ten to twenty-five cents. There were some eight or ten of these, and as many of them were crowded to the water's edge on some of their trips, it is fair to suppose that a handsome profit was derived. Probably no less than a hundred thousand pairs of eyes gazed upon the huge stranger in the course of the day. Yet, notwithstanding the throng, the dust, the heat, and other things calculated to try one's temper, the best of decorum prevailed, and the services of the large force of police were comparatively unnecessary. Lemonade and lager bier received liberal patronage, and some of the venders reaped handsome profits from the hungry and thirsty. A few instances of intoxication required attention, as they always do in a miscellaneous gathering; but nothing that came to our ears indicated that the general peace and good order had been disturbed. On shipboard everything appeared quiet. An occasional head protruded above the bulwarks and looked down upon the crowd, but no connection between the ship and shore took place except when some lucky fellow received leave of absence, when he moved as rapidly through the crowd as a joyful pair of legs could carry him. It is estimated that not less than fifty-thousand people visited the dock on foot alone, to say nothing of the great number who looked upon her majestic form from the decks of sundry steamers. Everybody appeared delighted, and expectation, judging from the various remarks, did not appear to be greatly disappointed."

This morning one of our quarter-masters named Durrell,

was found dead in his bed, his death being the result of constant intemperance. A wife and several children are in this case left nearly destitute. A coroner's inquest was held on the body, and the usual verdict returned. He was buried on the following morning, another victim offered up at the shrine of intemperance. On Monday morning a party of us, consisting of eight officers, having obtained the necessary leave of absence, and passes, which were kindly presented to us by the different railway and steam-boat companies, started at 7 A.M., with beautiful weather, in the fastest steamer in America, the "Daniel Drew," for Albany. The Daniel Drew left New York at 7 A.M., and after eleven stoppages on the way, arrived at Albany at 4·30 P.M., having performed the distance of 150 miles at the rate of nearly nineteen miles an hour.

After arriving at Albany, we took the omnibus and drove up to the finest hotel, "Delavan House," a magnificent building, sumptuously furnished; the entry of our names in the visitors' book was sufficient to ensure us every attention from the spirited proprietor, Mr. Loyselle, junior. After a little brightening of the outward man, we proceeded to replenish the inward with the good things of this life, and after satisfying the cravings of nature we sallied forth to satisfy those of curiosity. We visited the Capitol, or Senate House, a large, substantial, white stone building, with nothing particular to mark its exterior. The Assembly Room is a fine spacious apartment, tastefully furnished; a full length portrait of Washington overhung the seat of the chief magistrate. The Senate Chamber is somewhat similar, hung with portraits of American celebrities, with, to English eyes, the strange addition of a handsome porcelain spittoon to each desk. The Library, a large square room, contains 80,000 handsomely bound books, with a picture gallery; around which is an elaborately-worked iron railing. Albany, the capital of the Empire State, was founded by the Dutch in 1614, and received its present name in honour of James, Duke of York and Albany, afterwards James the Second, at the period when it fell into the possession of the British, 1664. The population is about 6500. The principal public buildings are the "Capitol," the "State Hall," the "City Hall," the "Hospital," "Penitentiaries," and between forty and fifty churches. The houses are well built, but the streets very irregular and ill paved. Before leaving we partook of a glass of champagne with the proprietor, who kindly insisted on considering us his guests, and as such would not allow us to pay a farthing. We gladly take this opportunity of returning our thanks to all for their kindness both on board the Daniel Drew and at Delavan House.

Left for Niagara at 11 P.M., by the New York Central Railway, engaging a berth each in the sleeping car. These cars are arranged with two tiers of side berths similar to a cabin in a small ship, being attached to all night trains in America. Each sleeping car is furnished with the necessaries for performing the morning's ablutions, although I cannot speak in high terms of the articles generally in use for arranging the hair, both comb and brush being securely chained to the side with so short a scope as to require the greatest ingenuity even on the part of a wide-awake Yankee, to put them to their legitimate use. About 7 A.M., stopped at the city of Rochester to breakfast, which was ready awaiting us in a large comfortable room; plenty of good things to satisfy good appetites, with both civility and attention as a relish, the charge made being only two shillings. Rochester is a large and important city, with a population of 45,000. The Genessee Falls lie close to the town; it was from Table Rock in the centre of them that the celebrated Sam Patch made his last and fatal leap in 1829. Having twice previously jumped into the rapids near the Falls of Niagara, and once from the Table Rock, the latter a height of 125 feet; he never rose after his last leap, his body never being found. During our trip by rail to Niagara, we passed through many towns, but of course it is useless from a mere passing glance to attempt a description of them; the country I should like to describe, but find myself unable to do so in the manner it deserves. Woods, fields of waving, ripening grain, rocks, rivers, mountains, and plains, are all blended in one grand picture, by that great painter, Nature. At 11.15 A.M. (after a ride of about twelve hours from Albany), we arrived at the Falls, taking up our quarters at the International Hotel. Had a delightful bath, which somewhat restored us, after our fatiguing journey, and then started in a carriage for the Falls, crossing the small suspension bridge on to Goat Island (on the American side); each person for this privilege being required to pay a fee of one shilling, and to enter his or her name in a book kept for that purpose: after having once paid your fee, you are free to cross for the rest of the season. This island is private property, and the source of a considerable income to its proprietor. The rapids, as seen from this bridge, are a grand and impressive sight; the rocks, which are in some places visible above the surface, seem tormented with some supernatural agony, and fling off the wild and hurried waters as if with the force of a giant's arm. After a ride of some few minutes, and crossing a small foot-bridge, we find ourselves on Luna Island, and standing on the very edge of the American Falls: the Horse-Shoe Fall being visible at the same moment.

To attempt to describe what we felt whilst gazing on this ceaseless, rolling, roaring world of waters, jumping madly down a height of 163 feet, stunning the looker on with its thunder, and blinding him with its spray, were useless; no pen could give an idea of the delight and reverence with which we gazed in speechless wonder at this sublime sight; it must be seen and felt to be appreciated.

> "Flow on for ever in thy glorious robe
> Of Terror and of Beauty: yea, flow on,
> Unfathom'd and resistless. God has set
> His rainbow on thy forehead, and the cloud
> Mantled around thy feet: and He doth give
> Thy voice of thunder power to speak of Him
> Eternally, bidding the lip of man
> Keep silence, and upon Thy altar pour
> Incense of awe-struck praise
>
> "Thou dost speak
> Alone of God, who pour'd thee as a drop
> From his right hand, bidding the soul that
> Looks upon Thy fearful majesty be still—
> Be humbly wrapp'd in its own nothingness,
> And lose itself in him."—SIGOURNEY.
>
> "And what are we,
> That hear the question of that voice sublime?
> Oh! what are all the notes that ever rung
> From man's vain trumpet, by Thy thund'ring side?
> Yea, what is all the riot that man makes
> In his short life, to Thy unceasing roar?
> And yet, bold babbler, what art thou to Him
> Who drowned a world, and heaped the waters far
> Above its loftiest mountains?—a light wave,
> That breaks and whispers of its Maker's might."—BRAINERD.

The spot on which we were standing was, on the 21st June, 1849, the scene of the following melancholy accident:—

The family of Mr. Deforest, of Buffalo, visited the Falls in company with a young man named Charles Addington. They were about to leave the island, when Mr. Addington playfully seized Annette, the little daughter of Mr. Deforest, in his arms, and held her over the edge of the bank, exclaiming, "I am going to throw you in." A sudden impulse of fear caused the child to bound from his grasp and fall into the rushing stream. With a loud cry of horror the young man sprang in to save her, and, ere the stricken parents could utter a cry, they both went over the Falls!

The Falls consist of three, the "American," "Central," and "Horse-Shoe," the last, and by far the grandest, being situated on the Canadian side, from whence the best view of them all is obtained. The first-mentioned fall is 163 feet in height, 660 feet wide; Central same height, 240 feet wide; and the Horse Shoe 163 feet in height, and 2000 feet in width. The waters running down from the great lakes (for which the Niagara forms the outlet) cover an area of 150,000 square miles; floods so grand and inexhaustible as to be utterly unconscious of the "ninety millions of tons" which they pour every hour, without ceasing, over these stupendous precipices. The term "Niagara" is of Iroquois extraction, and signifies the "thunder of the waters." Terrapin Tower occupies a singular and awful position; as the guide-book says of it, it appears to have "rushed in, as fools do, where angels fear to tread." About fifty feet from Goat Island are some small rocks, a few feet above the surface, with the water dashing madly over them. On one of these the "Tower" is built; it is of stone, very small, and about forty-five feet high, connected with Goat Island by a small bridge consisting of two or three planks laid from rock to rock, and this being constantly wet and slippery requires great care in crossing: from its summit the most sublime view conceivable presents itself, but it requires well-strung nerves to contemplate it calmly; the waters rushing onwards to their final leap, thundering and roaring as if they would carry both rocks and tower into the dread abyss (which stands within twelve feet of the extreme edge), making the stoutest heart quicken its beat, and the fiercest eye quail as it glances into the awful depths below. The Horse Shoe Fall is, as I have said before, by far the grandest of the three; it is computed by Professor Lyell that fifteen hundred millions of cubic feet of water pass over its edges every hour. A condemned vessel, the Detroit, was, in 1829, sent over this fall, and, though drawing eighteen feet, she did not touch the rocks in passing the brink of the precipice, showing there must be a depth of at least twenty feet of water above the ledge.

"Termination Rock" is a sort of cave formed behind the Horse-Shoe Fall, and reached by the descent of a built stairway. Before descending, visitors equip themselves in a complete suit of waterproof garments, and, being thus prepared, we descended the steps and followed our guide along a narrow and exceedingly slippery platform of rock close to the precipice, and with sundry misgivings in our minds as to the safety of the attempt; however, having heard that this feat has been performed by ladies, we determined to proceed, which we did with a quickened pulse, and breathing with great difficulty on account of the dense spray, which nearly blinded us. Quite deafened by the roar of the falling cataract, we pushed on, having been informed by the guide, before starting, that upon arriving at the "worst" we must get on as fast as we could, it being easier to get beyond the sheet of waters than to turn back; when we got inside, after a very fair idea of the sensation of drowning, what a sight presented itself! The outward bend of the falling water, and the inward curve of the precipice, form an immense cave; the sun, shining full upon the cataract, giving it the appearance of an immense mass of transparent moving crystal, the flying spray forming rainbows of many colours and in all directions completely bewildering the astonished beholder; but as now our position was anything but a comfortable one, and sundry misgivings as to our safe return presenting themselves before our excited imaginations, we retraced our steps as quickly as we could, feeling immense satisfaction at finding ourselves once more on "terra firma." Decidedly this undertaking is more pleasant to remember than achieve. We spent this day in gazing in increasing rapture at the wonders before us, and reluctantly left for our hotel, as night was dropping her dark mantle over the scene.

After supper and a good night's sleep, we rose next morning determined to witness the falls from the river. To gratify visitors in this particular, a small steamer is kept running up to the foot of the Horse-Shoe Falls every hour, or oftener if required. She is appropriately named the "Maid of the Mist," and is of 120 tons burden, and 100 horse power; she starts about two miles below the falls, two shillings being the fare, including the use of waterproof garments. After leaving the landing stage, we steamed toward the falls, the greatest care and skill being required in steering, in consequence of the eddies and ever changing currents; the little vessel steamed so closely by the "American" and "Central" Falls as to deluge us with the spray, and then steered boldly, as it were, into the very jaws of the foaming cataract, at the foot of the Horse-Shoe Fall; where, stunned by the thunder of the falling water, deluged and blinded with its sprays, we almost fancied ourselves doomed to destruction; but no; just in time the helm of the little vessel is shifted, and, aided by her powerful machinery, she darts, as it were, from the very jaws of death, leaving us to doff our oil-skins and wipe the water from our eyes, by which time we are at the Canada ferry; and in a few moments we find ourselves wending our way up the cliffs, hardly having had time to collect our scattered senses, with a deep and lasting impression of the great fall engraved upon our hearts. On ascending to the road, we find ourselves close to Clifton-house, a magnificent English hotel, near which the sanguinary battle of "Lundy's Lane" was fought. The view of the falls from this hotel is exceedingly fine, and being near the grand fall possesses for visitors many advantages over others, as well as the satisfaction of seeing the "Banner of Britain" proudly waving over your head. A pleasant walk of about half-an-hour brings us to the suspension bridge, a really noble structure, the work of Mr. John De Roebling, of New Jersey. It was commenced in 1852; it is of enormous strength, being calculated to carry over 12,000 tons; is all wire-rope, and, as a work of art, for strength, beauty of construction and simplicity, it stands unrivalled. Its height above the rapids is 250 feet, span (single) 800 feet, width twenty-four feet; the road for carriages and pedestrians is suspended twenty-eight feet below the railway line. The four large wire cables forming its principal support are ten inches in diameter, and contain 4000 miles of wire. The total weight of the bridge is 800 tons, its cost 100,000*l.* sterling; each foot-passenger, for crossing, with the privilege of returing the same day, pays one shilling; for a carriage six shillings. About a couple of hundred feet from the bridge, is the rope of the daring, but fool-hardy, Blondin: we saw the plucky little fellow cross, and perform all sorts of antics, over the boiling rapids. When he appeared, ready to perform his wonderful feat, the wind was blowing nearly a gale, and although entreated by many of those present to desist until the fury of the wind had somewhat abated, the dauntless man started forth upon the rope, heedless of the advice given him, and in a moment this was his only support as he moved midway between the yawning gulf beneath and the clouded heavens which spread above; and as he passed forward, his hair flying in the wind, with difficulty maintaining his position, a thrill of terror passed through the frames of all present: with the greatest trouble he proceeded along, the wind in its tempestuous fury almost sweeping him from his slight foothold. Already two or three guys had snapped through the force of the gale, but the undaunted Blondin continued his journey. He now reaches the centre, and calmly and complacently lies upon his back, and then, gaining a sitting position, balances the pole across the rope, and stands upon his head. He turns a somersault, and then resumes his walk for the Canada side. Here, not satisfied with the danger he had already undergone, he has his eyes blindfolded, and, getting into a sack, starts on his return. His agent on the American side trembled with fear, as he slowly and deliberately continued his hazardous journey. He is more than half-way over when suddenly his foot slips, he staggers, and then, without the slightest trouble, he once more sits upon the rope. The slip, as it appeared to us, was only a *ruse*. Once more he starts for the American side, and is soon received by a tremendous burst of applause. But I derived no pleasure from witnessing such a performance; for though I cannot but admire the extraordinary nerve and courage possessed by this wonderful man, it seems to be a desecration of a spot seemingly set apart for grave reflection ; it is no place for a mountebank performance. We visited M. Blondin at his own residence, in the village of the falls, and were introduced to his wife ; a good tempered, lively little body, with a pleasing face. Blondin himself is a small spare man, standing about five feet, with a cast in one eye, notwithstanding which his face is a pleasing one ; they have two or three children. Mrs. Blondin presented us with likenesses of her husband, and he himself with pieces of the rope on which he walks, with a written guarantee to that effect ; the rope is two inches in diameter, made of white hemp, called by sailors Manilla rope.

A few words about the International Hotel, and then I must reluctantly bid adieu to Niagara. This hotel is a most stupendous as well as an elegant structure, containing every comfort, a capitally served table loaded with the most *recherché* dishes ; but the most remarkable thing in the establishment is the excellent manner in which the waiters are drilled ; no confusion, but marching in and out with dishes in double files like soldiers, to the music of a band stationed in an orchestra in the upper end of the magnificent dining saloon. One peculiar feature is the manner in which the plates, &c., are placed upon the tables ; four waiters at each place themselves in a row, one having plates, another knives, the third forks, and the fourth spoons ; at the ringing of the conductor's bell, the band strikes up the march in "Norma ;" the waiters march round the tables keeping time to the music, their arms all going together, the four at the same moment depositing on the tables the articles they carry : it is really astonishing how quietly and orderly everything proceeds owing to this excellent system. After an early dinner and the settlement of our bills (charge 10s. 6d. per day board), we started in a carriage, crossing the Suspension Bridge for the last time, and stopping at the depôt of the Chippewa and Ontario Railway, having free passes in our pockets for a ride to the city of Niagara, fourteen miles distant, standing on the edge of Lake Ontario. This line of rail runs through a beautiful and well cultivated country. After a ride of about forty-five minutes, we arrived at Niagara, the terminus of the line ; and during the thirty minutes which we stopped, we visited the steamer Northerner, about starting for Toronto, and were much pleased with her excellent accommodation for passengers. Lake Ontario from its shores presents very much the appearance of an inland sea, being of great extent, and is ofttimes ruffled by severe storms. We returned by train as far as the village of Chippewa, there taking the steamer Clifton for Buffalo. On board this steamer was a return party of drunken Irish excursionists, who had been celebrating Orange-day at Chippewa: we had but little peace during our stay on board, for they were fighting the whole time. This trip by steamer has but little to interest; Chippewa, from which we started, is as far in the direction of the falls as steamers dare venture. Buffalo stands at the mouth of the Niagara, and, on the shores of Lake Erie, its distance from Chippewa is twenty-two miles. It was 7.30 p.m. when we arrived there, and we immediately went on board the lake steamer City of Buffalo: she is a beautiful model, her lines nearly similar to the Great Eastern, painted entirely white outside. Tonnage 2200 tons, and 340 feet long. On entering the gangway, the first thing that struck me as a novelty, on board ship, was a handsome marble fountain, playing, with gold fish swimming in the basin. The saloons, cabins, &c., were gorgeously elegant, surpassing anything of the kind I had ever seen before; the arrangements for passengers, &c., were perfect, and the vessel as clean as a new pin. At 8 p.m. we started for Cleveland on Lake Erie, distant 190 miles, arriving there at 7 a.m. the next morning, having travelled all night at the rate of eighteen miles per hour. Before leaving the city of Buffalo we partook of a hearty breakfast; then landing, rode off to the Angier House Hotel, and started thence to view the country. We were much pleased with the pretty villas and their nicely arranged gardens, &c.; we visited the celebrated "water cure" establishment, of which it is said in Cleveland that more whiskey is consumed there than in any hotel. The trees and shrubs, as we drove along, presented a very beautiful appearance, so fresh and green. This is the second city in importance in the state of Ohio, and boasts of a population of over 60,000; it is laid out with broad, well-paved footways, but the roads are very bad, the centres being principally formed of planks, in many places in a sadly dilapidated condition, very dangerous for horses. After enjoying a very pleasant day, and being treated with the greatest kindness by Mr. Taylor, the proprietor of the hotel, we started at 8 p.m. on our return by the same steamer, arriving at Buffalo at 7 a.m. next morning. The commander of the steamer, Captain Perkins, behaved towards us with the greatest kindness and courtesy, and would insist on treating us as his guests.

Upon landing took up our quarters at the Mansion House Hotel, and after breakfast went for a stroll through the town, and were much pleased with the size and construction of the buildings generally and the cleanliness of the streets; the principal one, Main Street, though not so long, I think quite equal in appearance to the Broadway of New York, and more deserving the name. The guide-books say of Buffalo (in 1858) "This important commercial and manufacturing city has grown so great and so fast that although it was laid out as late as 1801, and in 1813 had only 200 houses, its population now numbers 80,000 (so that it may now be calculated having at least 100,000 inhabitants!) it is an earnest of the wonderful progress we shall see by-and-by in the Western Cities." After a comfortable night's rest, we turned out at 8 A.M., had breakfast and another short stroll through the town, leaving by the 10.25 A.M. train on the New York and Erie Railway for Elmira.

Of the towns through which we passed it is useless, as I said before, from so cursory a glance to attempt a description; but as to the country, no pen can do justice to its beauty. For very many miles the track (to avoid cutting through the mountains) ran by the side of the rivers Susquehanna and Delaware, crossing and re-crossing them several times; the scenery on their banks is most beautiful.

At 5.30 P.M., after a lovely ride, we arrived at the sweetly picturesque town of Elmira,—a charming valley nest, with environing hill-ridges. Rode up to Haight's hotel, arranged our toilets, enjoyed a hearty meal, and then sallied forth in the cool of the evening for a ramble. After leaving the town (which is small and of no importance) we found ourselves surrounded by charming little villas, with here and there a good sized mansion, a small stream running by the road, putting us much in mind of the lovely scenery about Hampton Court, the sort of place a happy couple might fancy an earthly paradise.

> " A cottage in this fairy scene,
> Whose sheltering boughs seem ever green;
> The streamlet as it flows along
> Seems murmuring forth a fairy song."

This town is celebrated for its Female College, a very large and beautiful building, the lady pupils, studying for surgeons, lawyers, &c. What would our own "dear ones" of England think of an establishment of this kind? I think the "Maids of merry England" may be excused the endeavour to emulate their American cousins in this particular. I saw some pretty faces that would never do for surgeons, for I feel satisfied they would, if called in, do more harm than good to the patient; perhaps cure him of the tooth-ache, and leave him with a heart-ache that no skill could cure: still I should have no objection to being attended by a lady practitioner, for we all know Sir Walter Scott spoke the truth when he said of woman,

> " When pain or anguish wrings the brow,
> A ministering angel thou."

After enjoying a lovely moonlight walk we returned to our hotel thoroughly tired, and then to bed.

At 4 A.M. the next morning took our seats in the Cincinnati express train for Jersey City (opposite New York). Passed through some very wild mountain scenery, stopping at a town called Deposit for twenty minutes to breakfast, and after a ride of ten and-a-half hours through a well cultivated country, arrived at Jersey City at 2.20 P.M. Before leaving the train let me say a few words concerning the regulations on the different lines; the roads are well kept, time the same, and civility from the conductors the order of the day. There is but one class of carriages, or "cars" as they are called here, and they are open for communication from one end to the other, so that the conductor walks the whole length of the train, and gathers the tickets before arrival at a station, thus saving detention. He is also able to walk from the engine to the baggage van, giving him the opportunity of seeing all is going right in the different parts of the train, and consequently, this must add to its safety. Our own railway officials might adopt a somewhat similar arrangement with benefit to themselves and the public. After leaving the train we crossed in the ferry-boat to New York; drove down to the Great Eastern, and at 3 P.M. once more found ourselves "at home."

---

From Monday 7th July to this date, Monday 16th, 26,821 persons have visited the Great Eastern. A large fire occurred to day near the ship, causing the destruction of thirty-seven houses; three or four days back, a fire of even greater extent occurred, totally destroying a great number of small buildings, known as the Washington Market; one took place on the opposite side of the bay, the same night. Fires appear to be of very constant occurrence in this city, though I am informed the arrangements for their suppression are excellent; the greatest difficulty to overcome being the pugnacious disposition of the firemen belonging to the different engines. A week back, a sanguinary fight took place between them in this city, whilst proceeding to a fire, five men being shot, and several others wounded; this is rivalry with a vengeance.

The Chicago Zouaves (a small volunteer force) visit the ship by invitation to-morrow; they are thus spoken of by the "World."

"The nucleus of a Zouave regiment has been formed at Chicago, and it is now in New York attracting much attention. On Saturday, the Chicago Zouaves were reviewed by the Mayor, and went through their drill in the open space in front of the City Hall. Among the thousands who saw their evolutions, were many well qualified to express an opinion upon them; and the judgment of these critics, we believe, was highly commendatory. The nature of the evolutions, however, was such that any intelligent observer could see their object, and judge of their effect; and upon the mass of the spectators the impression was one of vivid pleasure. The endurance, the celerity, and the spirited movement of the Chicagoans, was no less commendable than their precision, intelligence, and skill in combination. They united, in a very high degree, mobility, flexibility, and power of concentration. They are a fine body of young men, about forty in number; and they appear to have a full supply of that nervous energy which enables the American to bear more, and work longer, as well as more intelligently, than men of other nations who have larger muscles. Their system will be closely studied during their visit; and ere long we may expect to see a New York Zouave regiment in full charge across the parade ground of Central Park."

*Tuesday, July 17th.*—Fine weather, but exceedingly warm. About 11 A.M. the Chicago Zouaves visited the ship, and thousands flocked to see them, it having been given out that they would go through their extraordinary drill on the quarter-deck; they however came without arms, much to the mortification of the assembled thousands.

The visit of a deputation from Philadelphia yesterday, for the purpose of endeavouring to persuade the directors to take the ship there, is thus alluded to by the "New York Express" this evening:—

"NEW YORK, *July 16th*—P. M.—The joint special Committee of Select and Common Councils of the city of Philadelphia,—consisting of Messrs. Stephen Benton, Henry Davis, and William Bradford, on the part of Select Council; S. H. Case, Chas. H. Cramp, and William H. Baird, on the part of Common Council; and Robert S. Reed and Lorin Blodget, on the part of the Board of Trade,—appointed to visit New York for the purpose of inducing the directors of the Great Eastern to visit Philadelphia, arrived in this city at noon, and were formally received by Capt. Vine Hall, on the Leviathan, with the utmost cordiality and delight. The committee were first courteously shown over the ship by Capt. Hall, and then proceeded to the captain's private apartments, where they were introduced to the officers of the ship. Mr. Benton, the chairman, said that, 'He felt happy in being the official bearer of the friendly resolutions of the city councils of Philadelphia to the gentlemen connected with the greatest mechanical enterprise of the age; and he felt assured that a favourable consideration of the invitation to bring the ship to Philadelphia would result in a substantial advantage to those whom the officers represented.'

"To this Captain Hall made a graceful response, in which he said that the facts and arguments would be fairly weighed and duly considered, and it would afford him the highest gratification if the ship could be taken to Philadelphia.

"The government coast survey charts were then laid before the officers, and an earnest discussion took place between the Philadelphians and the representatives of the Great Eastern. It was proved, conclusively, that ships with a draught of 25½ feet could be safely brought to Philadelphia, and the safe arrival of the Cathedral was quoted as the proof. The ship was brought to the city some months ago with the above-mentioned draught of water, being unable to get over the bar at New York.

"Captain Hall assured the committee, that if the channel was of the asserted depth, there would be no trouble in taking the ship round, and he seemed quite delighted at the assurance of the committee of the warm public interest felt in Philadelphia in behalf of the proposed 'coming of the Leviathan.' It was positively ascertained that the first difficult point in the navigation of the Delaware is the Hog Island Shoal, at Fort Mifflin, which is dangerous not only on account of the bar, but also the abrupt angle of the channel; but this can no doubt be safely got over.

"A chart of the river front was also shown, by which it was clearly established that the ship could be moored at any point on the river front from Kensington to the Navy Yard, in a depth of from 40 to 70 feet, at which Captain Hall was delighted, and said repeatedly, in his bluff, frank, hearty English way, 'It is a fine river—it is a fine river!' There can be no doubt of this, for with all the boasted superiority of the harbour of New York, the Great Eastern is lying aground at low tide. The maps and charts, together with the data and information carefully prepared in every point, were left with the officers at the captain's request, with the understanding that they desired another interview to-morrow (Wednesday) at twelve o'clock.

"The committee were highly pleased with the kindness of the captain, and they feel assured that it is already a fixed fact that the Great Eastern will visit Philadelphia. Many inquiries were made after well-known Philadelphians, particularly Captain James West, the 'veteran of the Atlantic;' and much delight was expressed on the part of the subordinate officers at the prospect of the visit to the Keystone city."

The Philadelphians were, however, doomed to disappointment; for it was next day settled, the risk being considered too great, not to attempt taking the ship there. Eight thousand persons visited the ship to-day, among whom were a number of excursionists from different parts. On the 18th, our commander, accompanied by the surgeon and second officer, left on a trip to

Niagara, the assistant-surgeon starting alone on a trip farther west. Ship, as usual, full of visitors from 8 A.M., till 7 P.M.; weather very warm. A New Yorker accosted me this morning with " Well, Mister, I reckon you've got a mighty fine ship here; I guess you've licked us this time." Another said, " There's a mighty sight of iron about this ' boat ;' but I guess we can build wooden ships: we want none of your darned iron in this 'free country.' So you had to come to America to get the idea how to build her; suppose you know you stole the lines from us." One old lady asked if the " donkey engines were not for conveying visitors about the decks, 'cause, if so, she guessed she'd like a ride." Questions of all sorts pour thick and fast upon us, and it requires great forbearance to treat all comers with civility, some questions reflecting anything but credit on the asker, and many being downright insulting. On the succeeding day, the directors officially announced, that the exhibition of the Great Eastern would positively close on Saturday, July 28th, and that she would positively sail for England, viâ Halifax, on the 16th of August next. In order to accommodate persons who desire to go on a short excursion, a trip to Cape May has been decided on. This will take place on Monday, July 30th; and on Wednesday, August 10th, the Great Eastern will return to New York. The fare for the two days' trip will be ten dollars, exclusive of refreshment, which will be provided on board.

About 10 P.M. last evening, a large ball of bluish fire was seen in the western sky, at an elevation of about 15 degrees; its course was about E. by S., and as it approached the meridian it burst, and then two reddish coloured meteors, with tails of streaming fire, with falling sparks, shot on towards the east; the velocity of these was about 20 degrees per minute. They travelled in line, and at an equal elevation, disappearing in the east in about two minutes after the phenomenon was first seen.

*Sunday, 22nd.*—Ship closed to visitors; weather very fine, photographers at work taking views of different parts of the ship. The Rev. C. M. Denison, minister at the Seaman's Chapel, held divine service on board, as also last Sunday.

*Monday, 23rd.*—Strong southerly winds and much rain, clearing up towards the afternoon; we have two bands playing for the amusement of visitors, one in the saloon, and Dodworth's (celebrated as the best in the country), on the quarter-deck. A great number of visitors on board this day, and on the succeeding one the astonishing number of 16,300 had a look at the big ship; they were principally excursionists. T. P. Barnum made an offer to buy up the whole of our Cape May excursion tickets (they are limited to two thousand), and pay 20,000 dollars in cash for them. The directors, however, very properly refused, determining to dispose of not more than five to any one person. The crowd on board this day was so great, as to render it a work of no little difficulty to get about the decks. The papers to day are full of accounts of the wonderful meteoric phenomenon of the 20th. In the evening I visited Mr. Barnum's American Museum, where, for the charge of one shilling, amusements of all kinds are provided, including a theatrical performance (a seat in the boxes being $7\frac{1}{2}d.$ extra), "curiosities," both living and dead, wax-figures, very fine and well-stocked aquariums, the "happy family" on a large scale; a living skeleton, lightning calculator, the Albino family, with pink eyes and long silky white hair, and last, though decidedly not least, a fat boy of seven years of age, weighing 257 lbs., and measuring 61 inches round the chest! This museum is well worthy a visit at six times the money. The visitors (as before, mostly excursionists), attained on the 25th the extraordinary number of 17,000. Visited, and had a long conversation with, the French giant, M. Joseph (exhibiting in a tent alongside the ship), from whom I learnt, that many years ago he was performing at some of the London theatres, and was well acquainted with the late Albert Smith, being then styled the Belgian Giant. He is 7 feet 8 inches in height, weighing 400 lbs., and is a man of immense muscular powers.

*Thursday, 26th.*—Were visited, by invitation, by a New York volunteer Militia company, formed entirely of Scotchmen, wearing the Highland costume. At 3 P.M. a heavy thunder-storm burst over the ship, and it continued to rain heavily up to 7 P.M., much to the discomfort of our numerous lady visitors, and the destruction of their extensive silks and crinolines. We did what we could to make them comfortable during the rain, giving up the use of our cabins to them : such attentions are by some courteously acknowledged, while others take them as a right. The word "private" over a door in England would be sufficient to keep visitors from entering, but not so here; some two or three blackguards in the face of that notice, entered the superintendent purser's cabin while that gentleman was balancing his accounts, and on being politely requested to withdraw, one of the ruffians unhooked a large picture in a gilt frame hanging on a panel and threw it at his head, smashing the picture to pieces. I might mention several outrages of the same kind, although some of the perpetrators did not get off without a "receipt" for their "politeness." The only notice taken of the ship to day by the press is the following :—

"LAST DAYS OF THE GREAT EASTERN.—About 17,000 persons visited the Great Eastern yesterday, filling the ship from the time of opening in the morning, until the gate was closed at night. Dodworth's band struck up some lively music in the afternoon, which gave much pleasure to the crowds that were present. Notwithstanding the extraordinary number of visitors, all inconvenience in seeing the various parts of the ship was prevented by men stationed by the officers to answer all inquiries, and by the new guide book, of which many avail themselves.

"The arrangements for the Cape May excursion are rapidly progressing, and from present appearances, the excursionists will be well provided for."

I am thus particular in inserting extracts from the different papers, as I wish the New Yorkers to speak for themselves concerning the Great Eastern, and to show how little it takes to turn the current of popular favour to a swift running stream in the contrary direction. On the following day (Friday), 18,000 persons visited the ship. Among them was one old gentleman, perfectly blind, who had come all the way from Wisconsin, purposely to "feel" the big ship. He was conducted round by some friends, and asking for an explanation of all he "felt." He appeared to derive considerable entertainment from his visit. At 7 P.M., great excitement was caused by observing a screw steamboat on fire at some little distance from the ship: it proved to be the "T. C. Durant." She left her wharf with fifteen passengers, including some women and children, and after getting into the river, a fire was discovered in the after part under the main deck, and near the boilers. The excitement among the passengers became very great; and the female portion ran about her decks screaming and acting in a frantic manner: in less than ten minutes the stern was enveloped in flames. The captain very wisely ran her on shore, and thus saved all lives. The flames were not extinguished till damage had been done to the amount of 5000 dollars. On the first alarm, three of the boats of the Great Eastern were manned and cleared for lowering, but the intention of the captain of the burning vessel to run her on shore being perceived, they were not sent, as the people were out before the boats could have got alongside. Blondin and his wife visited the ship, and dined with us to-day, being much delighted with all they saw. He expressed a wish to stretch a rope across our mast-heads, and walk from one to the other. I learnt from him, that while he was performing on his slack-rope over Niagara, three days back, his gold medal (presented to him by the people of Buffalo) fell from his breast into the boiling torrent below. "I felt inclined to jump in after it," said he; "but," turning to his wife, "I thought of you, my dear, so just stopped where I was." He seemed rather disconsolate at his loss, as he prizes anything of this sort very much. He intends crossing on stilts when the Prince of Wales visits Niagara. The "Herald" of to-day has the following:—

### "The Great Eastern.

"An immense crowd—eighteen thousand people on board—assault on one of the officers—American ruffianism versus English courtesy—the Cape May excursion—sleeping and eating—the Highlanders, &c.

"Reader, do you want to see a crowd? To be squeezed, reduced, contracted and epitomised, dovetailed and wedged in; to be scowled at by women and anathematised by men; to have your uninsured corn plantations remorselessly trod upon, and to groan in the very vexation of spirit thereat; to have parasols stuck in your eyes, and elbows in your ribs; your hat smashed, your bosom mussed, or if a female, your crinoline compressed into shapes so indefinite that geometry is defied to supply a name; to pay half a dollar for the privilege of being pummiced down by constant attrition against your fellow men (to say nothing of the women), and have an incomparable sweat-bath thrown into the bargain; to take your wife and daughter to see a show and be treated to intermittent glimpses of it between your neighbours' legs or over the summits of their heads? In a word, do you want to feel that you are nobody—neither a slice of lemon nor a lump of sugar, but an amazingly small drop of a compound mixture in which your natural identity is for the moment gone? If so, go on board the Great Eastern in these final hours of her visit to American shores.

"People often frequent public places, no matter whether the occasion be a sermon or a play, for the purpose mainly of seeing the crowd. To all such we say go and stand an hour near the passages of the big ship. We have mingled somewhat in the miscellaneous multitudes of Gotham, and have been reduced to dimensions smaller than nature ever intended, but in all our metropolitan experience we have never seen any gatherings from day to day to which that now daily coursing the decks of the big ship would bear any comparison.

"The Academy of Music in its palmiest nights is 'not a touch to it.' The Jenny Lind concerts, years ago, were only a circumstance, and so far as any other continuous entertainment can be mentioned, we do not remember an instance, when, to follow up our plebeian quotations, the crowd could 'hold a candle' to that which we have recorded as a part of the American history of the Great Eastern.

"We cannot afford a better illustration of the character of this throng than to suppose a couple of our popular churches stationed at either end of a short street, with their doors thrown open for the egress of a hungry audience about dinner-time. One of these would fairly represent the going and the other the returning throng. In this manner the excitement is kept up nearly the entire day. The climax is reached about two o'clock in the afternoon, but the stream of humanity continues its flow until four or five o'clock, before the diminution is really perceptible. Even then the decks are almost uncomfortably compact with visitors, by reason of the presence of Dodworth's band, and the music they daily discourse to the admiration of our country friends; but it is, nevertheless, a good time to make a tour of the ship. A still later hour, say from half-past five to seven, is preferable, however, for one can then look about without being subject to the annoyances to which we have referred.

"The number of visitors on board yesterday up to one o'clock, was not far from ten thousand, and from this time until about four they grew in numbers at the rate of two thousand an hour, until nearly nineteen thousand people had been recorded as having entered the ship.

"The heavy shower in the afternoon produced a little lull, but the scrambling on deck towards the lower regions to get out of the wet, was quite as bad in its collective and individual results as if several thousand people had been instantaneously added to the number. Notwithstanding this immense presence, every person was in due time favoured to his entire satisfaction with a complete view of the ship. Attendants were stationed at several of the companion ways to prevent the rush, and to dispose of the crowd as fast as it accumulated, while Mr. Bold, the general financial manager of the Great Eastern Company, and Messrs. Machin, Davis, and Wallace, officers of the ship, were unceasing in their efforts to afford proper facilities to all for enjoying their visit.

"There are some individuals, however, and we regret to acknowledge it, who do not seem to appreciate kindness, no matter how disinterested, and are always disposed, when they receive an inch, to take an ell. One of this sort yesterday unceremoniously entered the room of one of the officers. Supposing it to be a mistake, the latter courteously remarked that it was a private apartment, and not intended for exhibition. The fellow, who was meanwhile fumbling at some account-book on the table, savagely replied, he 'Didn't care a d—n what it was for; he had paid his money, and was bound to see all there was to be seen.' Being then ordered to leave the cabin, he seized a large glass frame containing one of the printed regulations of the ship, and with all his force threw it at the officer, and backed out. Fortunately it did not strike its mark, and more fortunately for the ruffian, the gentleman had the forbearance not to shoot him on the spot, as he had the means of doing, and as many others similarly situated would have done, or even to have had him arrested and punished as he deserved.

"In this connection, it may be added that there is not an officer attached to the Great Eastern who is not a perfect gentleman and entitled to gentlemanly treatment. They are courteous to our citizens and to visitors far beyond the ordinary requirements of civility; and if all the ladies and gentlemen who have visited the ship and been the recipients of their hospitality, were called upon to announce the fact, the record would show that they have not been a whit behind our own residents in bestowing those delicate attentions which so quickly knit the friendly tie, even upon those who have not the slightest claim upon them or an acquaintance that extends beyond the passing moment."

---

*Saturday, the 28th*, is the last day of exhibition prior to leaving for Cape May. The ship as usual very full of visitors from all parts of New York state. One lady, having three children with her, brought me a letter of introduction from Toronto in Canada; her curiosity must indeed have been great to have brought her all that way to see the Great Eastern, but I am ungallant enough to believe that the last new fashions in some of the Broadway stores had far more attraction.

The following is the register of visitors from the first day :—

| | | |
|---|---|---|
| First 5 days, at 1 dollar | . . . . | 8,578 |
| Second week, at ½ dollar | . . . . | 26,821 |
| Third    ,,    ,, | . . . . | 32,029 |
| Fourth    ,,    ,, | . . . . | 76,336 |
| Total | . . . . | 143,764 |

Having some conversation with a gentleman to-day upon the subject of "equality," I related to him this anecdote, which amused him very much. Whilst in London, chief officer of an East Indiaman, and lying in the East India Docks, I stepped out so far as the lock entrance to witness the arrival of a vessel of the same class just returned from Calcutta, called the Nile, the chief officer of which ship (an old friend of mine), in the pride of uniform and a safe return home after an arduous voyage, stood on the forecastle returning the salutes of his numerous friends (some eight or nine hundred people being assembled on Brunswick pier). Under the bow of this noble ship, and blocking up the entrance to the docks, was a lighter full of wet shingly ballast; the man in charge (an Irishman) was attired in a red cotton nightcap, a very dilapidated blue serge shirt, a pair of old dirty drawers and clumsy boots completing his costume: he was complacently sucking at a short black pipe. My friend hailed him from the deck of his ship, some twenty feet above, with "Get out of the way with that ballast-lighter, will you?" This, twice repeated, drew forth the following colloquy:—"Are you the captain of that ship?" "No, I'm not," was the answer, "but I'm chief officer." "Well," said Paddy, with the most provoking indifference, "spake to your aquals; I'm captain of this one!" Amidst the roars of laughter which followed this retort, my friend vanished.

There were many visitors from the country on board this day: the distant rural suburbs were well represented; foreign-cut coats, and antique shapes of all kinds of provincial habiliments were very conspicuous. Gentlemen with much more health in their faces, and less nap on their broadcloth, than is seen in Fifth Avenue, were also present in goodly number; while white-panted and loose-jacketed Great Easterns were swaggering about the decks; and the officers, evidently in excellent health, mingled their English rotundity of form with the fragile figures of the New York belles. At 7 P.M our visitors were all rung out, and the workmen commenced clearing away the entrance and exit gangways, and making other preparations for a move to-morrow.

*Sunday, 29th.*—Dull, cloudy weather, and showers, with strong S.E. winds. Commenced at 6 A.M getting on board moorings, anchors, &c.; and at 4.30 P.M., being high water, and steam ready, let go our fasts, and in the presence of eight or nine thousand persons steamed off from the wharf and anchored in the centre of the river, the whole operation not taking half an hour. The first revolution of our immense screw-blades brought to the surface the body of the unfortunate man who was drowned the night after our arrival; it was picked up, and after a coroner's inquest, was decently interred. It rained with great violence the whole night, with a strong wind from the S.E.

*Monday, 30th.*—The day appointed for our departure for Cape May was fine and warm, with but little wind. The excursionists, to the number of about 1500, commenced arriving at 1 P.M., in small steamers engaged for that purpose by the directors, and at 4 P.M. they were all on board. Two of the best bands procurable in New York, as well as our own, were provided for the amusement of the music and dancing loving portion of our friends. Extensive preparations had been made, and quite an army of black waiters engaged to attend to their creature comforts; and over a thousand mattresses bought, in addition to our already large supply, on which they might rest their wearied bones. Everybody anticipated a pleasant two days' trip: for once, everybody was mistaken; but I will leave the tale to the reporter of the "New York Herald," whose narrative displays none of the malice to be found in the other newspapers.

### "THE GREAT EASTERN PICNIC.

#### "THE DEPARTURE OF THE LEVIATHAN FOR CAPE MAY.

"TWO THOUSAND PEOPLE ON BOARD—THE SCENE IN THE BAY—THE ESCORT AND THE ENTHUSIASM—A NIGHT ON THE ATLANTIC—FUN, HUNGER, MISERY, AND MATTRESSES—AN INDIGNATION MEETING ON BOARD—AMUSING SCENES AND INCIDENTS—A MAN OVERBOARD—THE RETURN HOME, ETC., ETC., ETC.

"THE history of the Great Eastern has been one of epochs. Whether on the stocks or in the water, in the long process of a launch, or the scene of a life-destroying explosion, on a passage across the Atlantic, or as the focus of a multitude—from her conception until the present moment, the events that have followed each other thick and fast in her chequered career have partaken of the stupendous character of the big ship itself.

"The present excursion ought not to be excluded from this catalogue, for while it is no uncommon occurrence for a company, much greater in number than that now throbbing around me, to embark on a jollification jaunt to a distant place, never, in the history of this or any other country, has there been such a conglomeration of humanity, such a scene and such surroundings, as those which characterise this first pleasure peregrination of the colossal Queen of the Sea. As such, it is worthy of a place in the current record of the times.

"A trip to Cape May is an event of ordinary occurrence; but a trip in the Great Eastern is another thing; and when it was modestly announced in the journals of the day that she would proceed thither for the purpose of affording the public an opportunity of personally enjoying such a voyage, there were few hearts that did not pulsate in sympathy with the thought, 'How I should like to go.' One drawback, however, and a most essential one, too, prevented many from yielding to this first and strongest impulse. With that keen eye to the interests entrusted to their care which has throughout characterised the management of the big ship on the part of the directors representing the Great Eastern Company in this country, these gentlemen saw fit to charge, for the privilege of a two days' sail, the high price of ten dollars, exclusive of the keeping and necessary comforts of the voyagers. Naturally, every one commenced his arithmetical calculations. Here were four dollars extra for a berth in which to sleep, at least two dollars a day per head for the privilege of eating, an additional two dollars for a twelve hours' interval at Cape May, and sundry other miscellaneous incidentals, which would swell the expense well nigh upon twenty dollars. The result was, that for the entire week following the advertisement the utmost indifference appeared to prevail, and it was only now and then that one could be found in the whole community anxious to come forward and loosen his purse strings to the required extent. Up to Saturday night this number amounted to the insignificant figure of eight hundred, and the contemplated excursion promised to be a magnificent failure. The threatening weather of Sunday did not at all improve the financial prospect of the undertaking, and it was only when the breaking clouds of Monday, the culminating excitement of expectation, and the probabilities of a splendid trip, lent their convincing aid, that the public came forward and swelled the number to the limits which is is understood had been set by the directors, namely, two thousand.

### "THE EMBARKATION."

"As we have already stated, the Great Eastern hauled off into the stream on Sunday afternoon, and there, lying just opposite the mansion of Commodore Stevens, at Hoboken, she waited the arrival of those who were to compose her party. In order to accommodate the excursionists, two small steamers were provided, which, at intervals of fifteen minutes or thereabouts, ran between the ship and the foot of Hammond street, where they had been requested to assemble. Here, on our arrival, a busy scene presented itself. First, was the crowd, so dense that it was almost impossible to make one's way through it; then we stumbled upon a dozen or more carriages, bringing both visitors and lookers on; and, finally, on arriving at the edge of the dock, we came upon the little steamer that was to convey us on board. Three or four trucks were drawn up in close proximity to the boat, loaded down with mattresses, a part of the instalment ordered for the accommodation of the passengers, and these were being passed to the deck of the steamer. A pile of baggage lay on the wharf marked for Cape May and Philadelphia, which looked as though some Flora McFlimsey had judiciously selected the Great Eastern for her journey, and from one to two hundred individuals were dovetailed together in the little space allotted to passengers, anxiously waiting the termination of the loading process to which we have alluded.

" Patience soon found its reward, however, and in a few minutes we were ploughing the waters of the Hudson and alongside of the Great Eastern. To run up the side stairway, present our ticket to the officer at the gangway, pass the inspection of three or four detectives who have been engaged for the purpose, is but the work of a few seconds, and we find ourselves on board. A couple of hundred have preceded us, and carpet bags and trunks strewn around, indicate that their owners either have determined to come well provided with clothing and fodder, or that a large number purpose extending their journey from Cape May to other points. Several baskets here and there very plainly contain the good things of life, and though a smile was excited at the thought of 'bringing coals to Newcastle,' we have since had occasion to envy the forethought which led their owners to look out for number one before they started, rather than trust to the uncertain management of the providers on board.

"Only a few minutes pass before another steamer approaches. Its crowd of two or three hundred are discharged, and come hurrying up the gangway, as we did before them. Dodworth's band arrives, and the big fiddles and little fiddles, packages of music, and musical instruments that follow them, give promise of a rich treat to those who love the concord of sweet sounds. The load is discharged, the lines are cast off, and the little minnow of a steamboat drops astern to give place to another, and another, and another, until by two o'clock some two thousand people have been transported from the shore, and are promenading the deck, listening to the music, discussing the approaching excursion, or rambling in the abysses of the vast ship which has attracted them from their homes and business.

"It may be interesting to some to know the style of our ticket. It was about as follows, for we write from memory:—

---

EXCURSION TICKET.

STEAMSHIP GREAT EASTERN.

FROM NEW YORK TO CAPE MAY, AND RETURN.

Leaving New York, July 30, at 3 P.M.; leaving Cape May, July 31, at 6 P.M.

PRICE, TEN DOLLARS.

J. H. YATES, *Secretary.*

---

"The company having now fully arrived, we have an opportunity of looking around and seeing

"THE PEOPLE ON BOARD.

"It would be a task to name all of these, for they represent every class and condition likely to be present on an occasion of this nature. They come. too, from almost, if not quite, every State in the Union, as well as from many of the countries of Europe, to say nothing of Africa, which a score of dark-skinned waiters on board almost constantly call to mind. Millionaires, ministers, lawyers, editors, reporters, doctors, tradesmen, poets, artists, authoresses, politicians, gamblers, prize-fighters, and gentlemen at large, all pass in review, and give to the assemblage a cosmopolitan character which it could not possibly have in any city outside of New York. Quite a considerable proportion is composed of ladies, and, strange to say for such a gathering, there is not one observable on whom suspicion can for a moment rest.

"Messrs. Dickson, Young, Farley, Radford, and Duzenbury, detectives, and Captain Seabring, of the Ninth precinct, are also on board, and though their services have not as yet been required their presence has doubtless been valuable, on the principle that 'an ounce of preventive is worth a pound of cure.'

"It was amusing, however, to watch this variegated throng as they came on board.

"'Where's my state room?' was the universal inquiry, and invariably the first movement was in the direction of the imaginary place where they were to repose, or the imaginary individual who kept the keys to these Morphean recesses. Officers, servants, seamen—people of all others on the ship the least capable of imparting the required information—were buttonholed, annoyed and victimised by the impatient crowd, until they were almost hoarse with—' Go to Mr. B.'

"'Who's Mr. B.?'

"'The man with the blue ribbon around his hat and book under his arm—who is always taking snuff.' (We may also add that he is the financial manager of the affairs of the ship.)

"The result is that the brunt of these attacks fell upon the unfortunate gentleman whose 'blue ribbon' made him such a conspicuous mark of attraction. With a fund of pleasantry, however, which, like a shrewd politician he knew how to use, the pertinacious applicants were requested to wait until after the starting of the ship, and for the time he was left to enjoy his snuff-box and neuralgia in something like the peace he coveted.

"It was now about three o'clock.

"THE APPEARANCE OF THE CROWD.

"At this time it was interesting in the extreme. So far as numbers are concerned, they exceeded even those who witnessed the arrival of the Great Eastern. On both sides of the river, as far as the eye could reach, up and down, the shore was black with people. Housetops, hillsides, wharves, ships, barges, rigging—everything that afforded foothold to see the spectacle, was occupied. Immediately around the ship lay a score of steamboats, tugs, rowboats, and small craft, all loaded to the water's edge and waiting the departure of the ship. Owing to the perversity of the tide, however,

## "THE START

did not take place until after four o'clock. As we have before remarked, the Great Eastern lay with her head up the stream. In order to turn the gigantic vessel the steamtugs Achilles and Yankee were employed, but for more than half an hour after the huge anchor left its muddy bed—the largest by the way that ever rested on the bottom of the Hudson—they strove with might and main to bring her into proper position. The ship yielded gradually, however, and at a quarter to five o'clock the revolution of the paddles and the screw, and the long white wake behind, announced that we were fairly on our way to sea.

"The scene that now ensued is one that cannot be soon forgotten by any individual who witnessed it. The multitude of humanity was visible on every side. On shore the eye rested upon nothing but crowds, extending even back into the country as far as the vision could reach, and on the water eighteen or twenty steamers loaded to the guards, bedecked with colours, whistling their enthusiasm and thundering their salutations, glided along in the huge shadow of the Great Eastern as it trembled in the waters of the bay. We did not count all of these, but the following are the names of those recalled to mind at the present moment, together with the estimated number of passengers on board:—

| Keyport | 250 | Flora | 700 |
|---|---|---|---|
| Flushing | 400 | Columbia | 700 |
| Delaware | 700 | Paterson | 700 |
| Tiger | 400 | Francis G. Speight | 600 |
| Red Jacket | 700 | J. S. Darcy | 600 |
| Thos. Hulse | 300 | Hudson | 400 |
| Jas. A. Stevens | 400 | J. B. Frazer | 900 |
| Hendrik Hudson | 3,000 | | |
| Thos. Hunt | 500 | Total | 11,750 |
| Satellite | 700 | | |

"Onward we ploughed, passing the crowded Battery, the revenue cutter Harriet Lane, Governor's Island, Staten Island, the Narrows, and other places about which the story has already been told. Without, it is not difficult to imagine the appearance of twenty steamers, loaded down to the water's edge, constituting an aquatic escort, of which none could be a more worthy object than the noble ship upon which we are; while within and around us the excursionists have betaken themselves to every locality on the ship where they are not positively forbidden, to enjoy the spectacle. Some are in the tops, others are scattered through the rigging; many of the ladies have taken the platforms at the base of the wheelhouses, while the majority of the passengers are located along the bulwarks, standing on tiptoe, with their glasses peering at the ten thousand objects of interest around.

"The day is glorious. The ragged, threatening clouds have broken away in great masses, that are rolling off in the distance. The warm sunshine has tinged all nature with its loveliness, and the brightest anticipations of a pleasant excursion bid fair to be realised.

" 'THE BAR.'

"I do not mean the bar on board, but the bar off Sandy Hook, about which so many country editors have written the most fearfully discouraging leading articles. Little occurred during the sail down the bay worthy of addition to what has already been indited; but as we progressed towards the bar the interest among the passengers to see a locality about which so much has been said, led them to take places where they could command a view of the operations, and satisfy themselves by a personal inspection of the dangers of the place. Consequently they looked long and earnestly. They scanned the water with their glasses, then the bronzed face of pilot Murphy, then the captain, and then the water again; but we venture to say that few of them had any more idea of the real locality of the spot than did our Japanese friends of the constitutional morality of their Aldermanic confreres. The passage took place at twelve minutes past seven o'clock. The ship drew twenty-four and a half feet of water, and it is needless to say she went over without the slightest difficulty. The engines were 'slowed,' and a little more watchfulness was evident on the part of the officers, but aside from these incidental features of careful navigation, nothing occurred to indicate an extraordinary event. In fact, it seems to have been plainly proven that the Great Eastern may be as easily brought into the bay of New York as any other ship that has ever sailed in and out of it, and that the thousand and one stories respecting the absence of sufficient water and the dangers of navigation, are idle fabrications of the hour.

"At this point our escort left us. The little fleet of steamers that had been flitting about like so many flying fish, one by one dropped astern, parting cheers were exchanged, and the Great Eastern, alone and unattended, stood on her stately way towards her ocean-bound destination.

"The working of the massive machinery of the ship during this period was perfect. Nothing could have been more beautiful or wonderful. Without noise or jar—without even sufficient vibration to disturb the surface of the oil in the cups that revolve with the huge rods—the immense complication moved with a power that seemed almost supernaturally sublime. The ship likewise behaved admirably, and, though occasionally yielding to the long ground swell of the Atlantic, it was always with such gentle grace and easy movement that it was impossible to be so uncomplimentary as to succumb to even a single sea sick qualm. An hour or two later, however, we did see a few ladies and weakly gentlemen from the country, looking very much as if they could't help it; but the cause was doubtless due quite as much to their preceding carnivorous exploits as to the graceful undulations of the ship.

## "SUPPER.

"It was now what a sentimental miss would term 'the lovely and languid hour of twilight.' A majority of those on board had provided themselves with a hearty dinner before coming on board, but with a sea breeze in one's composition for six hours it is impossible to resist the pangs of hunger at some time, and the consequence was that as soon as the bar was passed a rush took place for supper that reminded us of the double quickstep charge of the Zouaves at the Academy of Music the other night. The simile might be followed up by the remark that they didn't enjoy a much better opportunity of doing execution. It was merely a charge 'at' and not 'into.' In other words, the feeding arrangement, from beginning to end, was a specimen of mismanagement and inexperience that might have been expected from some half civilised Hottentot, whose brains and taste had been used up in acquiring the little information he knew, but which one would not look for in any representative of that august body—the Great Eastern Steamship Company. The meals, and the manner in which they were served up, were hardly worthy of comparison with the style of 'Dotheboys' Hall.' In fact, 'Old Squeers' himself, merely minus his bowl of molasses, galvanised into life for the occasion, might, without a great stretch of imagination, have been seen strutting around his scanty boards, in the well developed rotundity of the provider of the ship, as complacently as if his tables groaned under the fat of the land. Perhaps they did, but the subscriber didn't see it. We thought to ourself that he would be an unlucky Lazarus who was compelled to wait for crumbs at the door of such a Dives.

"We shall not attempt a description. There was a good deal of spoon, some tablecloth, and a variety of incidentals pleasant to look upon, but as for the food, its appearance was as rare as a comet. The coffee gave out on the second round. It cost a fee of half a dollar merely to breathe the passing incense of a cup.

Chickens smelt all over of antiquity; ham was salt, beef tough; tongue was nowhere, and ice, of which several tons had been shipped in the morning, was said to have given out. In fact, a general famine would have overwhelmed all hands if the ship had been a meal and a half away from land. The waiters, too, were, with a few exceptions, rare specimens of their species. One of these exceptions—and we are glad to notice them—was the carver of the second dining saloon, who became so disgusted with the whole proceeding that he laid down his knife and cleared out in disgust. Another was a gentle old darkey, whose shaved head and gathered topknot made him look like a venerable edition of a Japanese. The passengers called him the 'Tycoon,' and scores of ladies and gentlemen are indebted to his impartial care.

"As for the rest, they were a set of unmitigated rascals. They would lie, cheat, steal your chairs, and almost your money. We heard one asked by a gentleman for a cup of coffee. 'All out,' was the reply. 'Go and get a little for my lady, won't you?' 'Go to hell,' was the response, *sotto voce*, and the villain went off, with a mad flourish, as if he was going to tear the kitchen down. Others were perfectly blind and deaf, metaphorically speaking, to all inquiries, and it was only when their palms were scratched with the evil root, which they did not hesitate unblushingly to ask for, that they seemed at all to comprehend that they had been industriously requested to obtain a desired article of food.

"Wines, soda, and other liquors have been sold in large quantities; but I must say it, to the credit of the two thousand people, that I have not yet seen a single individual in a state of intoxication.

"A very judicious arrangement, had it been successfully carried out, would have been the publication as follows, of

THE SCALE OF CHARGES FOR REFRESHMENTS ON THE GREAT EASTERN.

| | | | | |
|---|---|---|---|---|
| Tea and coffee, per cup | 6 | Claret, quarts | | $1 50 |
| Ham and Beef, per plate | 25 | Sandwiches | | 12 |
| Ham and chicken, do. | 30 | Veal and ham patties | | 12 |
| Tongue, do. | 25 | Beef à la mode | | 25 |
| Ices | 15 | Biscuit and cake, each | | 6 |
| Mint julep, per glass | 12 | Lager bier, per glass | | 10 |
| Sherry cobblers, do. | 12 | Brandy, gin, rum and whiskey | | 12 |
| Claret, do. | 12 | Cider, ½ pint | | 25 |
| Milk punch, ⅞ glass | 12 | Champagne, quarts | | $2 00 |
| Iced milk | 10 | Do. pints | | 1 25 |
| Cocktails | 12 | Sherry, quarts | | 1 50 |

Soda water, lemonade, cream soda, sarsaparilla, each, 12 c.
To prevent mistakes, passengers are requested to pay on delivery.

"For the first two hours at dinner by this means every individual succeeded in having himself waited upon, received his dish full of pabulum, or rather the *quantum* prescribed, paid for it, and travelled. At present, however, they seem of little more use than so many pieces of useless table furniture, and for practical purposes are laid aside. People are eating whatever they can get. One of my neighbours at a table said a few minutes ago that he had had four consecutive rear ends of chickens in two meals, and was then at work upon the fifth, with a view to test a sixth, and continue the experiment until he had definitely ascertained whether or not any other part of that biped's anatomy had been brought on board.

"If the question was asked, to whom does the blame belong? I should say the provider, head steward, or caterer of the ship—a person by the name of C—. By a contract with the company he retains the privilege of feeding all persons on board the ship, from director to visitor, at certain prices, which are mutually fixed. I was informed that two or three others were also engaged with him in the speculation, and between them all they have succeeded in leeching the public to an extent they will never enjoy again. They have neither the ability to plan nor the tact to execute, and as far as regards providing for the wants of two thousand people in the rough and tumble manner they have set about, it would have been quite as wise to have made a miscellaneous mixture of all that was to be eaten and drank in one big pot, divided a spoon among the multitude, and told them to go at it. Mr. C— may be a good man personally. We don't know him. He may have very excellent intentions, a benevolent disposition, and a strong constitution; he may be punctual in his church attendance, reliable in his domestic duties, and unimpeachable as a citizen; but, notwithstanding all this, to-day has fully demonstrated that whatever may be his other virtues of head, heart, or person, Mr. C— 'can't keep a hotel.'

"THE NIGHT ON BOARD.

"How shall it be described? It requires the brush of the painter more than the pen of a writer. In fact, the scene is not to be described. While I indite, men and women are preparing to 'turn in,' with such accommodations as the ship affords. But, notwithstanding the thousand extra mattresses provided, the careful arrangements that were supposed to have been made concerning the disposition of the state-rooms, and the boasted facilities of the big ship for carrying any number of passengers, more than one-third will fail to secure anything on which to lay their head but the iron walls of the vessel, a coil of damp rope, or what sailors call the 'soft side of a plank.' It is about eleven o'clock. The people in the saloons, especially gentlemen accompanied by ladies, are frantically flying from pillar to post, first in search of Mr. B—, then of Mr. Y—, and *vice versâ*, until these gentlemen have got into such a sweat in their efforts to accommodate, that they have had to shut themselves up in their state-rooms to cool off. Something has gone wrong. The state-rooms have either got mixed, or the people have, and the result is that a man occasionally finds himself in one place and his wife tucked away somewhere else. Many who have paid for berths have been deprived of them entirely, and take their chances with those who have trusted to luck and disposed of themselves in regular camp style.

"The picture of the saloons from stern to stem—for everything is reckoned backwards in this ship—is something like the following:—First is the bar, now covered with saturated tablecloths, broken glasses, and empty bottles. Next a couple of the dining saloons, in which the waiters are hurriedly clearing away the *débris* of the day's work. Then we approach the ladies' saloon. Entering here we see on one of the velvet sofas a brace of children spread out at length, their mother watching over them. Individuals are lying under the tables and scattered promiscuously around the floor. The same scene is repeated in the forward ladies' saloon, with the exception that more ladies compose the tableaux, and make a considerably wider spread. None of them have coverings other than their own shawls; and the melody which their sonorous snores create might well have suggested the idea of an Eolian harp. It is hot and oppressive, however, and we hurry out

## "ON DECK.

"Here we get the *crême de la crême* of this midnight somnolescence. The sleepers are stretched out in all sorts, styles, shapes, forms, angles, and conditions. They emphatically lay around loose, looking very much as if they had been poured out of some big bag in a state of dilution and left to settle. You can begin to describe them anywhere. Some are packed away on the tops of the cabins, some are lying close alongside the bulwarks, some are sitting bolt upright, reposing obliquely, and stretched out on the straightest horizontal. Two individuals, more enterprising than the others, have sewed themselves between two mattresses, and are trying to nap it; but every now and then some joker sits down on the bulging pile and educes a series of groans and maledictions that would wake the seven sleepers. A New York reporter and one of the detectives—a very fat one by the way—have quite sensibly crawled into a sheep-pen for the purpose of being undisturbed: but a party of promenaders have discovered their retreat, and for the last ten minutes they have been trying to provoke the wrath of the caged individuals to see whether the fat man can get out.

"A speculative individual mounts the pen and exhibits them as wild animals, in a strain something like the following:—

"'Here, gentlemen, are some of the most extraordinary freaks of nature—animals that won't live upon the land and are bound to die in water. We have to feed 'em on seventeenth proof whiskey, which one man shoots into them with a double-barrelled squirt gun, while another holds their legs—a most interesting spec-ta-cle. Only five cents, and the refreshments thrown in. Feeding time in fifteen minutes.'

"A great crowd gather around, and the sport that ensues is immense. The reporter begs to be let out; has got lots of work to do; is in a great hurry, and make any quantity of excuses, but they don't 'take,' and a battery of conversation is fired off between the besiegers and the besieged. Among the visitors is George Wilkes, who, after a good laugh, ventures to inquire, 'Who put the animals in there?'

"'The directors,' was the reply.

"'Can't you get out?'

"'No; they've fastened us in.'

"'How do you like your pen?'

"'The pen,' says the fat man, in a deep ventricular voice. 'In my opinion, sir, the pen is mightier than the sword.'

"'Ha! ha! ha! he! he! he! ho! ho! ho!' cachinnate the crowd, at this witticism. 'Three cheers for the fat freak of nature,' which are given with a will.

"'How often do they feed you?' says one.

"'Hain't been fed at all.'

"'Call the directors! Here's a case of starvation,' cries an individual on the outskirts.

"'No; get 'em something to eat,' responds another. Forthwith a chap starts down the gangway, and, though it is midnight, in five minutes returns with the carcases of two Great Eastern chickens.

"'Where did you get them?'

"'Found 'em under C—'s bunk.'

"'Good for him.'

"'Hungry?' inquires the chicken man, as he temptingly rubs them across the bars near the noses of the victims, like the keeper of a menagerie.

"'Yes, of course we are.'

"'Can you smell it?'

"'Yes, it's good and strong. Put it in here.'

"'Well, growl! if you want it.'

"'Ugh h-h-h,' growl the 'animals' in the most capacious and artistically bestial manner, and amid the cheers and laughter of the crowd. The menagerie is fed, accordingly, the chicken being passed in on the end of a long pole.

"Somebody passes in a drink to wash the solids down, and the fun increases.

"Here, again, are family groups. A wife is tucked in between two settees, and the husband sleeps crosswise. Another chap has a table turned upside down, and is snoozing at a two forty pace between the legs. Here are more piled away like mummies in the most unimaginable places possible, which only would enter the conception of a sleepy man. In short, from stem to stern, there is a row of beds and bodies which give the scene an appearance like that of a hospital filled with the victims of some prevailing epidemic.

"Of course, in such a party there is fun—plenty of it. One group especially appears to be the centre of attraction. Three or four of the number are stretched out on their mattresses in the centre of the deck, while the crowd stand in a ring around them, and join in the laugh, the song or repartee. After a while one is introduced to make a speech, but, being unaccustomed to this work, he invites what he calls one of his 'Zou Zous,' whom he styles the 'Prize Baby,' to do it for him, whereupon the Prize Baby is received with cheers, and proceeds to publish to the crowd his diet, which he says consists of four hard boiled eggs and a blackberry three times a day, in soap and water (applause and laughter). This effort evidently finishes him, and he introduces his friend, 'Signor Mickey Farina, the celebrated Italian tenor, the greatest living artist of the age.' The tenor responds, in 'sweet Irish brogue,' by a touching melody, which he denominates 'a parody on the Dutch cheese.' Another is introduced as 'Col. Bobolinkibus, aid to Gen. Garibaldi in the Mexican war,' and requested to 'turn around and show his honorable scars,' which are of course behind. As the capillary substance on the summit of his head is exceedingly brief, somebody proposes 'three cheers for the man with the sand-papered head,' which are given with a will, and the military gentleman subsides upon his mattress. So the jokes go round. Everybody is good-natured, and witticisms fly thick and fast in every direction.

"It would require half a page to record the amusing incidents connected with this party alone. The 'beasts' were poked up with long poles, while the people cheered, shouted, yelled, hauled the cage around, squirted water with the hose, and raised the Old Nick generally.

"ONE O'CLOCK.

"Some persevering individual has cured Dodworth's man of his ails and aches, and the string band are on deck, making music for a score or so of dancers. They are all men, however, and as a 'stag' affair, now and then interspersed with gymnastics and mattresses, it is irresistibly funny. The ladies seem as lively as a brood of canary birds with long tails, and though they do not indulge in the sport physically, their merry ringing laughter endorses the amusement as beyond reproach. Somebody has just proposed a mattress race, and hardly are the words out before fifty men, with beds on their backs, have started off on a scrub match by moonlight. How it terminates of course it is impossible to see, but there is an amount of jollity in the occasion sufficient to stock a dozen ordinary parties of a similar kind. An hour or so of this active exercise soon wears them out, however, and by three o'clock the whole group, in fact the whole deck, is in a state of profound slumber.

"I was informed that at about two o'clock one of the mattresses was discovered to be on fire, owing to the careless distribution of a segar, and for a moment it threatened to endanger the rigging. It was extinguished, however, by a few buckets of water, without alarm to any one. It would be difficult for fire to make much headway, for hose are laid fore and aft on deck ready for instant use, and not even a segar is permitted below the main-deck.

## "FOUR O'CLOCK.

"Night's candles begin to burn out, and the twilight gray in her sober livery to mark the footsteps of the approaching dawn. The heavy dew of the night, mingling with the cinders from the smoke stacks, has converted the deck into a huge mud puddle, and the faces of unconscious sleepers are black and sticky with the dirty damp. Hats, coats and garments in a dilapidated condition are scattered around, and the scene is one that Hogarth might well have immortalised.

"By six o'clock the sleepers are nearly all up, but a sorrier looking set of 'human forms divine' our eyes never rested upon. Mad, tired, stiff, sleepy, dirty and sticky, with hair and eyes full of cinders, they get off their individual mattresses like so many fretful porcupines. And now another chapter of the mismanagement is developed. There is neither water to wash nor drink. Complaints come thick and fast. One man has paid a dollar for a basin full; another gratefully bestowed a quarter for a glass of ice water, which he barely obtained, while two or three reporters came from the nether regions, looking as pale and languid as if they had been drawn through a succession of brush fences. They say that somebody will have to suffer for it, and if one may judge from their manner, their matter, like Jersey lightning, will kill at forty paces.

### "THE MOVEMENT OF THE SHIP.

"During the night the paddle engines had a pressure on their boilers of twenty pounds of steam, and the wheel was revolving twelve times per minute. The screw boilers had the same pressure, and the screw was revolving thirty times per minute, the combined pressure of which was giving the ship a speed of about thirteen knots per hour. Every half hour the look-out men might have been heard calling from their stations, and at four o'clock the heaving of the lead indicated the depth of water to be twenty-four fathoms. The ship was then headed westward, and then was experienced for the first time the heavy ground swell, which made it difficult for one unaccustomed to the deck of a ship to maintain his equilibrium, and for ever set at rest the notion, if such was ever entertained by any individual on board, that a ship can be built large enough to resist the swell of the ocean.

"The ship arrived off Cape May about seven o'clock, having stood so far out to sea during the night as to be delayed a little beyond the time when it was expected she would make anchorage.

### "AN INDIGNATION MEETING.

"During the morning an indignation meeting was held on board on the quarter deck, in which Mr. William Filmer, of Brooklyn, officiated as Chairman, and Dr. John Howe, of New York, as Secretary. The following resolutions, drawn up on an empty stomach and with unwashed faces, were submitted and passed with a will:—

"'Whereas, from the previous reputation which the Great Eastern and her officers had established in the United States, the gentlemen and ladies who embarked on the excursion to Cape May, expected, and had a right to expect, decent accommodation and proper attention; and as it had been announced that she was capable of carrying an almost fabulous number of passengers, and affording them proper attention and accommodations; and

"'Whereas, we, the passengers on this excursion to Cape May, have been grievously disappointed in every expectation; therefore,

"'Resolved, That we, the passengers to Cape May, have been not only disappointed, but swindled; that there was no water to wash with, no towels to wipe with, and no berths provided, and many ladies were obliged to sleep in the cabins; that there was not a glass of water to quench their thirst, and that the whole arrangements were contemptible and disgraceful.

"'Resolved, also, That we will advise our friends who propose to go to Norfolk and Annapolis in the Great Eastern to stay at home for fear of similar treatment.

"'Resolved, That these resolutions be published in the "Herald," "Tribune" and "Times."

"'Signed by J. C. Perry, Brooklyn; David Sandford, Amsterdam; H. S. Decker, Reuben Burkhalter, New York: Alexander Matheson, Ogsdenburgh, N. Y.; Abraham Khlos, Malone, N. Y.; Sidney W. Hopkins, J. J. Richards, New York; John Brush, Paterson, N. J.; A. Reckless, Redbank, N. J.; E. C. Russel, W. S. Baker, J. L. Jewett, New York; John Howe, M.D., and fifty others.'

"It is proper to add in this connection that neither of the executive officers of the ship, from Captain Hall down, had anything to do with this mismanagement complained of, except in giving play to a laudable spirit to right, as far as lay in their power, a most perceptible wrong. Messrs. Machin, Davies, Smythe, Wallace, Wood, Cary and others, made every effort to accommodate the dissatisfied and unprovided passengers, and most of the night was spent by these gentlemen in going from place to place, routing out intruders, and securing berths for those to whom they rightfully belonged. Ladies were accommodated as far as possible; but many were forced to lie in the saloons and on the decks.

"The directors, Messrs. Gooch and Yates, and Mr. Bold, gave up their state-rooms, and slept themselves on the floor, manifesting in every possible way a desire to render every one comfortable, and correct the confusion which had resulted from the want of proper experience.

"Had the eating arrangements been of the right character, and Mr. C— done his duty effectually, the excursionists would not have said a word about the sleeping department; but to be doubly inconvenienced was more than human nature could bear without reaction, and hence the meeting and resolutions. A man's stomach sometimes requires the most careful handling.

### "OFF CAPE MAY.

"The Great Eastern lies about six miles from the shore, and it has been ascertained that we have run nearly fifty miles out of the way—at least such is the report. The programme advertised is to take the excursionists on board to the beach free of charge, and bring them back, a steamer being provided for the purpose. About half-past nine said steamer came alongside, and some seventy of us, who pushed through the throng waiting at the gangway for a similar opportunity, at the risk of neck and limb, leaped on board.

"Most of these seventy went to Philadelphia from the Cape, preferring to go home by that route than to trust to the exigencies of another night on the ship, and no doubt numbers of others will do likewise.

"On shore the greatest excitement appears to prevail.

"The beach is thronged with spectators; the two platforms extending out into the channel along which the steamers run to land passengers are also crowded; while up the road, as far as the eye can reach, the clouds of dust that rise in the air and sweep off to the eastward, mark a steady increase. Vehicles of every kind and condition incident to Jersey plantations, and born of Jersey ingenuity, are tied along the fences, gathered in clusters, or are moving along upon the beach. We hire one of these, with a party, at a quarter each, and ride 'up town,' or rather to the village—a distance of two miles. On the road the string of carriages is like a procession. In the village we find everything capable of holding humanity crowded to the eaves. Strangers and country people have been pouring in for the last twenty-four hours, and for ordinary mortals it is a matter of impossibility to eat or sleep.

"By invitation of Messrs. Laird and Woolman, however, of the Columbia House—the largest on Cape Island—we proceed there to secure the comfort denied us elsewhere. Thanks to the kindness of these gentlemen, we are afforded every facility for writing —a very important feature to us by the way—while a single meal brings out in striking contrast the wretched fare to which we have been subjected.

"As the day advanced quite a large number of the New York excursionists were added to our company, the principal object being the enjoyment of a good dinner and a glorious bath in the surf, which the sandy nature of the atmosphere and the heat of the day made a decided luxury.

"From this point, about two miles from the landing, the great ship was barely visible, her outlines showing dimly and indistinctly on the edge of the horizon, and her masts bearing semblance, in the distance, to a diminutive section of a thinly planted hedge fence in winter. Opera glasses bring her in closer contact to those who are looking from the windows of the hotel, and the same curiosity exists, on a smaller scale, which marked her advent in the bay of New York.

"THE EXCURSIONISTS FROM CAPE MAY.

"Little occurred during the day on either ship or shore specially worthy of notice. The boats J. L. Shrever, Jas. A. Warner, Delaware, Balloon, and a number of others whose names do not occur to mind, came from Philadelphia, and other points on the bay, with passengers, and landed them upon the ship. The entire number of visitors was between four and five thousand. The idea had been extensively circulated among them, however, that the Great Eastern would not arrive at Cape May, owing to an accident which, it was telegraphed on Monday evening, had occurred on board while lying in the bay. This, several of the excursionists said, had its effect in raising a doubt, which resulted in the comparatively small number of visitors present. About one hundred persons availed themselves of the opportunity to visit New York in the big ship, the fare from Cape May being placed at five dollars. Numerous tickets were sold among the crowd on the wharf by the New Yorkers, to whom I have referred as being thoroughly disgusted. These went off at prices ranging from two to four dollars, and one individual was so impregnated with the feeling, that he gave his ticket away for a ten cent. piece with a hole in it, which he says he shall put a string through to preserve as a souvenir.

"Great difficulty was experienced in getting people on board the Great Eastern from the steamers, because of the long ground swell that prevailed. The side stairways were crushed almost beyond redemption by the steamers alongside surging against them, and the leaping and dodging of those who went on board, to get on the gangway, was in some instances perilous in the extreme. The best of nature animated the crowd, however, and barring a little impatience on the part of each one to get ahead of his neighbour, nothing threw a shadow over anybody's heart.

### "A MAN OVERBOARD.

"On one of these occasions, just previous to the arrival of the James A. Warner, a man was seen to plunge from the wheelhouse in the water below. For a moment breath was suspended at the startling incident, but on rushing to the side the individual was discovered striking out for the wheel, in a cool and reckless manner, and order was restored. It is not known whether the man fell or jumped; but, from his manner, it is supposed that he made a leap merely for the purpose of lionising himself.

### "THE RETURN.

"At half-past six the people on the Great Eastern had the satisfaction of hearing the order given to get under weigh, and the operation of raising the anchor at once became an interesting relief to the monotony of the day.

"At eight o'clock we were well under way, bowling along at the rate of thirteen knots an hour. Salutes were exchanged with the steamship State of Georgia, bound outward; and as both vessels were travelling for a short time in one direction the opportunity was afforded of comparing the superior speed of the Great Eastern, which ran away from her competitor with as much ease as a man would outwalk a child.

"Supper was a little improved. The waiters have had a talking to, and Mr. C— has likewise received admonitions of a storm about his ears, which have added an additional wrinkle to his corrugated brow. An instance occurred during the day which shows the root of the trouble, and how little the management of the ship have been able to control the operations of this 'autocrat of the dinner table.'

"Some of the directors desired to dine at a certain hour with a small party of friends. The meal was accordingly ordered in the usual way, Mr. C— being the caterer; but, notwithstanding, two hours and a half elapsed before they succeeded in effecting their object. Then it was only done through the perseverance of one of the directors, who, with his own dignified hands, went and helped himself.

"It will be seen, therefore, that these gentlemen are not entirely to blame for all the deficiencies experienced, and that when they cannot help themselves it is impossible for them to help others.

"AT NIGHT.

"The night was lovely. Dodworth's Band set the dancers in motion, and for two or three hours the scene by moonlight was as delightful as one could wish. Many people, including several ladies, were compelled to lay out on the deck again, and as the air was cool, the breeze fresh, and plenty of cinders blew about, their position was anything but comfortable. More quiet prevailed, however, than last night. The jokers are fagged out, and are sleeping as soundly as their more serious neighbours.

"Below, early in the evening, the saloons assumed more of the form of a family circle. Parties were gathered in knots telling stories or indulging in reminiscences of the trip, strolling up and down the spacious rooms, examining the long row of a dozen or more photographic groups of the officers of the ship presented to the company by Gurney, or engaged in a quiet game of cards. By eleven o'clock, excepting a party of singers astern on deck, all was quiet; and by twelve 'God Save the Queen' and the 'Star Spangled Banner' closed the performances of these midnight minstrels. Most of the reporters were to-night accommodated with berths, and are in better humour than they have been.

"WEDNESDAY MORNING, *Aug.* 1.

"We are cutting the waters of the bay at the rate of twelve

knots an hour. The chief engineer tells me that during the night the ship made fifteen. I learn, also, from one of the officers, that she came near running down a large schooner, and that it was only by good luck, after the ship had stopped and backed water, that a collision was prevented.

"A number of persons from Philadelphia, who came on board at Cape May, were brought away by accident and turned up this morning. They express themselves as highly delighted.

"Breakfast was but a repetition of the meals already described. Mr. Minturn, jun., a son of one of the consignees, told me that he had paid a dime for a glass of water and two shillings for his mattress, so that no favouritism was complained of by him at least.

"The day is so fair and beautiful, however, that there is little disposition on the part of any one to grumble, and every one looks back upon the trip to Cape May as one on which they have enjoyed a share of fun among the changeful vicissitudes of the occasion sufficient to compensate them for all the misery experienced.

"Several steamers have come out to meet us bound off with excursionists, and, on a small scale, we have a repetition of the scene of Monday. Salutes are exchanged with the revenue cutter and one or two other craft, and at about ten o'clock anchor is dropped off the foot of Christopher Street, where the Great Eastern will rest until this afternoon at five o'clock, when she starts on her trip to the South.

## "THE OPERATION OF THE ENGINES.

"The following is a statement received from Mr. McLennan, chief engineer:—

"'The engines, both screw and paddle, worked admirably. No accident of any kind occurred to them. On the trip to Cape May the paddle engines made 9873 revolutions—the indicator of the screw not working. Thus the distance travelled was about $166\frac{1}{2}$ miles. The knots averaged about twelve per hour, or of statute miles between twelve and thirteen. On the return home the paddle engines made 8849 revolutions—thus travelling, as will be seen, some twenty miles less than in going out.'

## "AN INCORRECT IMPRESSION.

"The statement has been generally made through the city that the passengers on board the Great Eastern were supplied with their fare by Mr. Stetson, of the Astor House. As such a supposition is calculated to injure the reputation and business of any person with whom it is connected, after the occurrences recorded on the above excursion, it is desirable that the public should know that the gentleman above referred to had nothing whatever to do with the matter."

---

Of course, in the above account, allowance must (as sailors say of a new rope) be made for stretching. The mountain has been in labour to bring forth a mouse. As far as the directors of the great ship are concerned, all right-thinking persons will at once acquit them of blame, for of course their province did not lie in feeding a hungry mob; but many of them were out for a two days' spree, and ready to have a row about anything, or at anybody's expense. As to our provider, some little mismanagement may lie at his door; but much of his trouble, and the cause of many empty stomachs, lay with the excursionists themselves, for I saw much food, on its way to a table at which sat a hungry group in joyous anticipation of a good feed, torn by main force from the hands of the waiters who were carrying it, such brutish conduct of course making it impossible to give any degree of satisfaction to the many, who thus suffered from the inexcusable conduct of the few. As to the black waiters, they were a set of incorrigible blackguards, and no doubt practised the extortions complained of to its fullest extent, and many were without doubt insolent and inattentive. I saw several myself in a state of intoxication when their services were most required; but every endeavour was made by parties in authority to allay the rising bile of our friends: that we did not succeed is partly owing to their desire to be all served at once, and partly because, considering themselves as having cause for grievance, they were determined not to be satisfied. But enough has been said on this unpleasant subject. Doubtless, had the Great Eastern been an American ship, we should have heard less about such a paltry grievance as the discomfort of an excursion party; however, it taught the Americans one thing, that, in spite of all their talk to the contrary, John Bull can build a steamer, and sail her too. They are evidently dissatisfied with us for beating them on their most tender point (ship-building); therefore, having been the innocent means of hurting their feelings, we can forgive them for being riled.

I find it necessary to retrace my steps to say a few words about this Cape May, that has thus suddenly achieved notoriety from the visit of the Great Eastern. It is situated at the extreme southern point of New Jersey, where the Delaware Bay joins the sea; it is famous as a fashionable summer resort, possessing good bathing and hotel accommodation, and is distant from Philadelphia some 100 miles. Some five or six thousand persons from that city arrived by excursion steamers during our stay, to have a look at John Bull's big boat, as they call her; and what with them, and our excursionists from New York, the scene of confusion the decks of the Great Eastern presented was something terrible, and right glad were we when, after an immensity of trouble, and a perfect Babel of confusion and noise, we got rid of all strangers, lifted once more our ponderous anchor from its bed, and steamed away at the rate of seventeen miles per hour from Cape May. A few Philadelphians availed themselves of the opportunity presented them to take a trip to New York, at the rate of five dollars per head.

I need scarcely say we were delighted when the ship was once more anchored at New York (9.30 A.M. August 1), and the last excursionist, cursing as he went, had disappeared over the side. The quiet that now reigned on board was an enjoyment indeed to us, who for two-and-a-half days had been in a perfect uproar; we availed ourselves with right good will of the few hours given us to clean the ship, and by evening we were once more clean and decent. The heaps of broken furniture, and the damaged state of our beautiful saloons, bore striking testimony to the gentlemanly conduct of our late badly treated and much aggrieved fellow-travellers. To-morrow we sail for Hampton Roads, and thence to Annapolis, a present of 1000 tons of coal being the inducement to visit the latter place.

*Thursday, August 2nd.*—Fine weather; the papers are full of letters from our late excursionists, abusing in round terms ship, directors, and officers, for nothing in particular but everything in general. Not supplying them with a sufficiency of ice-water appears the principal grievance: truly something cooling would have done them good; however, it is to be hoped they will all cool down in good time. They have now an opportunity of which they have been long desirous, and right good use do they make of it, to abuse the Great Eastern and all thereunto belonging. When 1 speak of abuse, I allude to the numerous minor publications of New York, which abound in most scurrilous articles; use being made of language that proves one thing, and one thing only, that the writers are most consummate blackguards. We were requested, as officers of the ship, to answer some of these articles, which we did with our compliments to the would-be editors, "that we, as the boy did when the ass kicked him, took it from whence it came." Messrs. Phillips and Nash of the "New York Illustrated News," De Fontaine of the "Herald," Osbon of the "World," and others, have ever treated us with kindness and consideration, and kept the papers with which they are connected free from such malicious abuse as fills the dirty columns of such trash as "H——'s

Weekly," the "C——r," &c. Weeds such as these should have no place among the blooming flowers of the New York press: they should be plucked up and cast into the fire.

Lord Lyons, the British ambassador, honoured us with a visit this morning, and was received by Captain Hall and the officers of the ship. Captain Hall conducted his distinguished guest over all parts of this magnificent vessel; after a stay of about two hours we landed his lordship in one of our boats, much pleased with his visit. 5 P.M.—Fine weather: commenced shortening-in cable. We have on board 105 passengers, at the low charge of six dollars for the trip to Hampton Roads, and eight dollars to Annapolis, exclusive of provisions. At 6.10 P.M., the ship's head being the right way, up anchor and steamed leisurely down the Bay. On heaving our eight-ton anchor up to the bow, found that it was badly broken in two places in the shank (near the stock): condemned it as unfit for further use. This run down the Bay presents a striking contrast to the last; the only vessel that noticed us was the Cunard steamer, Asia, which ship fired a gun and dipped her colours as we passed, the Great Eastern returning the salute by lowering her ensign and firing four guns. Not one steamer was there to accompany us; no crowds of people lining the shores to see us pass; in fact no more notice was taken of the Great Eastern than of any ordinary vessel,—something quite novel in the history of the big ship. Our last excursion has evidently riled the Yankees, and they'll no more of us. Then, for a short time, good-bye sweet city of fires and pistol practice, and away to seek a welcome from our friends of the south. At 8.10 P.M. crossed the bar, and steamed away gaily, with fine weather and smooth sea. Till late at night all was jollity and hilarity; dancing was kept up with great spirit, a vocal and instrumental concert in the saloon adding to the general good humour prevailing. By midnight the decks were clear, and all but the watch enjoying sweet repose. The engines as usual were in excellent working order, and the Great Eastern was cleaving her way through the water at a speed of seventeen miles an hour during the whole night.

*Friday, August 3rd*, dawned on us with fine weather, light winds, and smooth sea; our passengers in high good humour with the ship, the treatment and accommodation they received, and expressing in the warmest terms their admiration at the arrangements and capabilities of this wondrous vessel. 3 P.M., observed the land on the port bow, and at 6.15 P.M. anchored in Hampton Roads, having steamed from New York, a distance of 340 miles, in 23 hours. On anchoring we fired four guns to announce our arrival, after which the Fort honoured us with a salute of 11 guns, which we immediately returned by hoisting the American ensign and saluting it with 13 guns.

Before arriving, the passengers held a meeting in the saloon and drew up a prettily worded letter of thanks, which they presented to our worthy commander, expressing themselves highly pleased with their comfortable passage and the courtesy that had been extended to them by him and the officers of the ship: a strange contrast this to the indignation meeting of our last trip. Some three or four small steamers, and a dozen or two sailing craft, freighted with the sight-loving public, were awaiting our arrival in the bay, and welcomed us with hearty cheers, and "God save the Queen" from the bands, our musicians playing "Hail Columbia," &c. The point off which we are anchored bears the name of Old Point Comfort. Nearly in the centre of the bay a large fort is in course of construction, on an artificial island; and on Point Comfort, commanding the roads, is situated the largest fort in America. There is also a naval hospital here.

The roads, in which the U.S. frigate, Brooklyn, and several small vessels were anchored, affords no shelter from easterly winds. There is but one hotel here, and but few other buildings. Hampton is famous only as a resort for parties of pleasure, invalids, and those seeking an invigorating air; the fishing is also very good. The James's river is navigable at a depth of twelve feet as far as Richmond (the capital of Virginia), 140 miles from Hampton. The town of Norfolk is eight miles distant, standing on the banks of the Elizabeth river, which is navigable for small steamers. We had no sooner anchored than a deputation of gentlemen from Norfolk came on board, inviting the captain and officers on shore to partake of Virginian hospitality; which invitation was declined with thanks; our stay here being too short to admit of its acceptance.

*Saturday, 4th.*—Fine, but very warm. About 9 A.M. visitors by steamers and boats of all kinds from Richmond and Norfolk were fast arriving, and by noon some thousands of gaily-dressed people of both sexes stood for the first time on the decks of the Great Eastern. Among those privately admitted were the Secretary of War, the Secretary of the Interior, and several Naval officers. On leaving we honoured the first-named gentleman with a salute of fourteen guns, which, as an exercise of common politeness, ought to have been answered by the frigate Brooklyn; but the Americans had none of that "commodity" on stock, or rather to waste on a "Britisher." The ship was all the afternoon pretty well filled with visitors, but at 5 P.M. there was a sensible decrease in their number. We had several slaves on board during the day, and they appeared well clad, well fed, and clean. I did not enter into conversation with them for fear of giving offence to their owners; for the American slaveholders are well acquainted with our ideas on the slavery question, and therefore would rather we should leave their "Niggers" alone. It is very amusing to hear the Americans down South abusing their brothers of the North, and *vice versâ*, concerning the "Slavery question." The visitors numbered to-day 4020.

Two pilots for Annapolis came on board *Sunday* the 5*th*, at 4 A.M. Commenced heaving in cable at 5 A.M. The steamers came alongside with a few passengers for Annapolis at the low rate of 3 dollars per head. 6 A.M., our eight tons of iron being once more at the bow, steamed out of the bay; at 7, stopped and discharged the Hampton Roads' pilot; and at 8, we were off Cape Henry, with fine weather and smooth sea, ship steaming gallantly ahead at the rate of seventeen miles per hour. We are now in the waters of the famous Chesapeake Bay, which extends as far as Baltimore, about 190 miles. On our way we passed several vessels, the crews of which lustily cheered us as we steamed by; two steamers came down from Baltimore crowded with people to meet us, and, as the advertisement had it, to accompany us up to our anchorage; they had the presumption to try their speed with us, but by the time we anchored a faint line of smoke on the horizon marked their "whereabouts." We anchored at 5 P.M. in seven fathoms water, six miles from Annapolis, in the state of Maryland. The other side of the bay is about ten miles distance, so that we are anchored nearly in the middle, there not being sufficient water to allow us to approach nearer the town. From Cape Henry, which we passed at 8 A.M. to our anchorage, is 155 miles, the whole distance being steamed in nine hours, at over seventeen miles per hour. The rivers Potomac, Susquehanna, and others, find their outlets in this beautiful bay. Baltimore is distant about forty miles, and approached from the head of the bay by the Patapsco river. This day has been exceedingly warm, the night close and sultry, with much forked lightning.

*Monday*, 6*th*.—Ship opened to visitors. The gift of coal, which induced the authorities to send the ship here, being partly the offering of a company owning what is called the Bay line of steamers, the right of conveying passengers to the ship is granted to their vessels, to the exclusion of others. These boats run during the day, at intervals of about three hours, from six in the morning till six in the evening. The visitors to-day numbered only 2500; but we shall doubtless have an increase. The charge for a return ticket from Baltimore is one dollar for the steamer and half-a-dollar for admittance on board the Great Eastern. The railway between Baltimore and Annapolis is also running several excursion trains daily, a steamer being employed by them to take visitors from the trains to the ship. This railway also runs to Washington, the political capital of the United States, and we shall no doubt have many visitors from there and other towns on the road. The weather during the day has been most oppressively warm, scarcely a breath of air stirring. Six vessels containing coals are alongside, and busily discharging, but as the big ship takes in her coal at large side ports near the water, it causes but little annoyance.

On the 7*th*, the weather was still fine, but the heat intense. The coaling is going on but slowly, as the men do not appear in working humour, and not particularly pleased at working in the heat of a tropical sun. The steamers from Baltimore and Annapolis came alongside to-day, well filled with visitors of all classes, —and I may well say "*all* classes," for there were ladies and gentlemen, pickpockets and rowdy boys, and blacklegs, each party well represented. The latter mentioned blackguards were the cause of much annoyance and trouble to us during the whole time of our stay; assaults were constantly going on. Only to-day a mob gathered round the bar, making a great noise, and being very properly refused drink, the ringleader knocked down one of the officers of the civil department, and the whole then pitched into the waiters in the saloon. This being a free country, these blackguards of course made use of their boots and teeth. However, the tables were soon turned; for some of our men, hearing what was going on, fought their way to the field of battle, and British blood being spilt, all that remained in the bodies of the pugilists was in a state of ferment, and the consequence was that an indiscriminate fight took place, and these scum of the American Backwoods received so many striking proofs of the necessity of a retreat that they were forced—some of them Bowie knife in hand—to make what Jack calls a "stern-board;" *i. e.*, clear out with their faces to the enemy, or rather what could be seen of their faces, for I feel satisfied that for many days some of them were quite safe from arrest by the police on any individual charge, so complete was their disguise. One of the blackguards, more ferocious than the rest, we put, hands and legs, in irons, much to the disgust of himself and friends. The ringleader of the mob, after this *melée*, grossly insulted an American lady in the presence of her husband, who at the time said nothing, but landed in the steamer with his wife's insulter, and when on the wharf took a revolver out of his pocket and shot him dead. This happened in the presence of several of our men, and much to their horror; but these summary acts of vengeance are common in this country.

At 6 P.M., Messrs. Davies and Wood, two of my brother officers, and myself, kindly accompanied and franked by our good friend Nash, of the "New York Illustrated News," and taking our band with us, left for Annapolis by the steamer, proceeding from thence to Baltimore by a train crowded to excess. An instance of the free-and-easy style of these people was shown by many of them climbing to the top of the engine-tender, some sitting on the wood with their legs hanging over the sides, at the imminent risk of being thrown down from the jolting of the carriage and killed. I, in my innocence, ventured a remark as to the danger of such a proceeding, receiving as an answer from the conductor, "I guess if they get chawed up 'taint no fault of ours." Owing to the crowded state of the train, we did not arrive at Baltimore till 9 P.M. On reaching the house of our kind friend Mr. Wm. E. Bartlett, we mustered our band outside, and made the streets echo with "The Star-Spangled Banner." As may be expected, we were not long in gaining admission, and found a snug bachelor party assembled to meet us, the salute of honour being imitated in a most agreeable manner to us thirsty souls by the popping of champagne corks. A good supper was on the table, consisting principally of crabs, for which this place is famous: there were crabs devilled (the meat being taken out of the shell to undergo this operation, and afterwards returned), soft crabs fried in cream, ditto fried in their natural state, and many others too numerous to mention. These crabs are considered a delicacy; they are eaten shells and all, and are of about the same consistency as a firm jelly. Being very hungry, we made sad havoc among the shell-fish, our appetites assisted by the reckless manner in which our friend Bartlett fired away with his champagne battery. After supper, and a dessert, consisting of the most luscious peaches, &c. the band treated us to some excellent music. Towards midnight we were joined by Marshal Kain (the head of the Baltimore police), and one or two other gentlemen. The evening passed as pleasantly as the kindness of our worthy host and his friends could make it, and at 2 A.M., after winding up like true Britons by singing "God Save the Queen" (the toast, "Her Majesty," having been proposed in a neat and complimentary speech by the Marshal, and responded to in true English style with nine times nine and a hearty "God bless her!"), we sallied forth, accompanied by all hands, to the Maltby House Hotel, and at about 3 managed to get to bed, merely to be, as far as I was concerned, the victim of some hundreds of bloodthirsty mosquitos. At 8, rose and dressed, having borne my inflictions with anything but quiet resignation, breakfasted, and paid a visit to the terminus of the Baltimore and Ohio Railway, the finest building of the sort I have yet seen in this country. We were kindly received by Mr. Woodside and other officials, and by them conducted to the dome, from whence, at an elevation of 150 feet, we enjoyed a fine panoramic view of the city. One great peculiarity that strikes the eye is, the long streets of houses, all of red brick; in fact there appears to be hardly any other material used for house-building. The public buildings generally are stone or marble. Baltimore, in the state of Maryland, is one of the four great eastern cities with a population of 250,000.

The Washington monument is a very fine piece of workmanship, the chief amongst its kind in the United States; its base is 50 feet square and 20 feet high, supporting a Doric shaft 177 feet in height, which is surmounted by a colossal statue of Washington 16 feet high. It is built of brick, cased with white marble, and cost 40,000*l*. Battle Monument, also of white marble, 52 feet in height, was erected to the memory of those who fell defending the city in September, 1814. Many of the public buildings are large and elegant structures, particularly the Exchange, which has colonnades of six Ionic columns on its east and west sides, the shafts of which are single blocks of fine Italian marble of admirable workmanship. The churches, benevolent and literary institutions, &c., are generally well built, and many of them imposing structures. The Catholic cathedral boasts of the largest organ in the United States, having 6000 pipes and 36 stops; it is ornamented with two excellent paintings —viz., the "Descent from the Cross," and "St. Louis burying his Officers and Soldiers before Tunis." This town is famous for the swift class of vessels here built, and known as "Baltimore clippers." Having expressed a desire to inspect the celebrated cigar steamer, we were favoured by the originator and builder, Mr. Winan, with a letter to Captain Vaughan, requesting him to afford us every information concerning this extraordinary vessel. After a drive of half an hour, we alighted at Mr. W.'s private yard, and stepped on board. We were kindly received and shown through the vessel by the captain and Mr. Winan, jun. Mr. Winan, sen., was formerly an engineer by profession, and is possessed of immense wealth, the perfection of his novel idea being amusement for him. The term "submarine" would also well apply to this vessel, for she is constructed to go either through the water or on its surface; the idea being, that instead of, like an ordinary vessel, mounting over a sea, she will pierce her way through it. She is formed like a cigar, being hollow, and pointed at each end, for the purpose of offering as small an amount of surface as possible to the assaults of the waves. She measures about 300 tons, is 235 feet long, works to 350 horse-power, and carries 200 tons of fuel; her diameter is 16 feet in the centre; the deck, from the form of the vessel, is confined to the breadth of a few feet and about half her length, with a substantial hand-rail to save persons from slipping overboard. She is entirely iron, and is propelled by a wheel placed in her centre, set with twelve propeller blades, which traverse entirely round the outside; and to allow the connection of this wheel with the engines, the vessel is divided in two, having sufficient space for the machinery, but so strongly secured together as to make this particular part of the ship the strongest. The wheel is so covered in as to prevent any water going below. She has a rudder at each end, 40 feet from the extremes, in the shape of a flat square shovel, projecting entirely clear of her bottom, and steering her with the smallest movement. There is an anchor at each end, formed like a sugar-loaf, large end down, intended to hold by its weight alone; each is hove up by a winch into a recess formed in the ship's bottom to receive it, and made of corresponding size and shape, so that when the anchors are up they are so fitted in the bottom that no part projects. Near the centre a small iron tower rises to the height of 15 feet, and is provided with strong glass, resembling ships' scuttles, through which the look-out can see a-head when the whole of the hull is immersed. I dare say some day we may hear of her making a successful trip across the Atlantic. Mr. Winan informed me that, to test her qualities, he anchored off Cape Henry till a gale of wind set in, and then steamed out against it, making 14 miles per hour, with scarcely any motion. To clean the bottom of this sea snake, it is only necessary to pass two chains round her, taking them to winches on shore, and thus to roll her over as you might a barrel.

During the afternoon we paid a visit to the immense establishment of Messrs. Gail and Ax, the largest tobacco factory in the States. By the courtesy of the proprietors, we were enabled to witness the whole process of tobacco, cigar, and snuff manufacture: that of cigars is carried on by hand; that of cutting tobacco and pounding snuff, by steam machinery. All the men employed in this extensive establishment (and I believe some of the women) were smoking at their work; and it struck me that from such inveterate smokers (constantly inhaling not only the smoke of tobacco, but tobacco itself, in the shape of dust) that a valuable opinion might be obtained of the effect of smoking on the human system. All the *employés* have permission to smoke as much as they please on the premises, but not to carry tobacco or cigars away. Some of them avail themselves of this, and smoke without ceasing the whole day through. One of these men, whose first waking thought in the morning was for his pipe, and who frequently finished the day by going to sleep with it in his mouth, died some few months back at the age of eighty-six, after being many years in the establishment. The general opinion of the proprietors and others able to give one is, that the use of tobacco is not injurious. We enjoyed another fine view of the city from the top of this splendid edifice. A violent thunder-storm, with heavy rain and vivid lightning, broke over the town, lasting for half an hour, cooling the heated atmosphere, and rendering the evening delightfully pleasant.

At 6.30 P.M. started for the Great Eastern in one of the steamers returning for excursionists left on board. I think I never in the East or West Indies found the heat greater or more unbearable than it has been the last day or two.

Arrived on board soon after 8 P.M., and found 1700 excursionists awaiting the steamer's arrival; and such a squeezing and fighting to get on board, such yelling and screeching; it really was wonderful how this immense throng transferred itself from one vessel to the other in safety. All the ship's officers were in attendance, and most indefatigable in their exertions to render service, especially to the ladies; they being treated with but little civility by an American crowd. After one or two cases of fainting, a few torn coats, scratched faces, &c., the majority got on board the small steamer in safety; some few of the more timid preferred to remain on board the "big ship" all night. These were provided with sleeping accommodation, and made as comfortable as circumstances permitted. President Buchanan has notified his intention to visit the ship to-morrow.

Coaling ship goes on night and day, with not very favourable results, the coal vessels being sometimes obliged to sheer off to an anchor to avoid swamping alongside.

*Thursday, 9th.*—Light fog and cloudy in the early morning; clearing away as the sun gained power, the latter making its appearance with every indication of a piping-hot day, which it turned out to be. Visitors commenced flocking on board in great numbers from 8 A.M., and the different parts of the ship were soon filled with a well-dressed multitude, amongst whom was a goodly sprinkle of ladies, many of them fine-looking women, and a few positively handsome, all gathered together to welcome the President. At 10.30 A.M. the presidential party were observed approaching (in the small revenue steamer, Anacosta), and were soon alongside, welcomed by twenty-one guns from the Great Eastern. Our commander and his officers were in attendance at the gangway to receive the distinguished visitors, and amidst the hearty cheers of the assembled thousands, the bands playing "Yankee Doodle," President Buchanan stepped on board the Great Eastern. He was accompanied by his niece, Miss Harriett Lane, some few members of the Senate, &c., some naval officers, and a large party of ladies and gentlemen. We (the officers) had all the honour of a separate introduction to the President, each being received with a cordial grasp of the hand, and a hearty " Glad to see you, Sir."

Mr. Buchanan is a venerable-looking gentleman, perfectly white headed, and over six feet in height, wearing the ordinary American dress and straw-hat, without the slightest distinction. Miss Lane, the niece of the President, is about the middle height, slightly inclined to *embonpoint*, very lady-like in her manner, about twenty-eight years of age, and decidedly good looking: for the benefit of our lady readers we will say, she was dressed in (what I considered) decided good taste—plain, neat, and good (my knowledge of millinery is far too limited to allow me to attempt details). After a minute inspection of the ship, the distinguished party were entertained by Captain Hall and the directors at a sumptuous *déjeûner*, served in the ladies' saloon. After a stay of two hours, Mr. Buchanan and suite left the ship, again shaking hands with the commander and his officers, expressing in warm terms the pleasure he had received from his visit.

Before leaving, Mr. Buchanan was presented with several little *souvenirs* of the great ship, with which he appeared much pleased. After the steamer had left our sides, we again saluted with 21 guns, which were returned by the Anacosta. It was rather strange for an Englishman to hear (as we did to-day), the head of a great nation accosted by the crowd in this style: " Well, Mr. President, how d'ye do? glad to see you; guess you're looking spry," &c.

The visitors began to thin about 4 P.M., and by 8.30 P.M., the last had cleared out. Some of our gentlemen (?) visitors take a delight in passing insulting remarks. One to-day, accosted me with " Mr. Officer, I guess this ship's a great humbug." " That's the opinion of every fool that's seen her," replied I. The Yankee moved off.

*Friday*, 10*th*.—Fine weather, ship full of visitors from 9 A.M.; coaling going on, still badly. At 3 P.M. got up steam in the auxiliary engines, and hove in forty fathoms of cable. Towards evening a bit of a swell rising, all the coal-lighters broke adrift, thus finishing our coaling in a most unceremonious manner. We should, if possible, have taken another 1600 tons: but not being able to do so here, it will be necessary to coal afresh in New York. By 7.30 P.M. all visitors out of the ship, awning furled, and all ready for sea. During the night it blew very hard from the N.W., with heavy rain, compelling us to again give the ship the cable we had previously hove in.

*Saturday*, 11*th.*—Fresh N.W. wind, with dull cloudy weather and rain. At 4 A.M. commenced (with steam and hand power), heaving in our enormous bower cable, the anchor not being up and secured, owing to the strength of the wind, till 6.50 A.M., at which time, under charge of two pilots, we made a clear start for New York, with thirty-four passengers at twenty dollars, including provisions. After a speedy run down the beautiful Bay of the Chesapeake, at 3.50 P.M. stopped off Cape Henry to discharge our Annapolis pilots, having made an average speed during the run of $16\frac{1}{2}$ miles per hour. One steamer came out from Hampton Roads full of people to see us, giving us a " good-bye." At 4.5 started a-head full speed for New York. The night was dull and cloudy, with a strong head-wind and occasional showers.

*Sunday*, 12*th.*—Light winds and fine; the land in sight on port beam; passing a number of coasting vessels. Mustered the ship's company at 11.30 A.M., and at 11.50 stopped abreast Sandy Hook' light-ship, after averaging a speed of sixteen miles per hour since leaving Cape Henry. Have to wait till three P.M. for high-water to cross the bar. Advantage was taken of this opportunity to get the ship's head on with known objects on shore to correct compasses. Three P.M. set on easy, and at 3.45 crossed the bar once more in safety. Steaming up the bay, but few boats came out to meet us; as before, our appearance caused no excitement among the New Yorkers. Returned salutes from two " Cunard's" steamers as we passed, and at 5.45 P.M. anchored near the old spot. The next day set in with a gale of wind from the S.E. and rain; at eight A.M. commenced taking in coal from barges, it being hoisted in by "horse" power. The cost of coal put on board is 25*s.* per ton. Ship opened to visitors, but owing to the inclemency of the weather very few came on board; between four and five P.M. the wind chopped round to the N.W., accompanied by heavy rain for several hours.

*Tuesday*, 14*th.*—Still blowing heavily from the north; owing to the unfavourable state of the weather had but few visitors. The following extract is from the " Herald" of this date:—

## "The Great Eastern Steamer.

"THE MAMMOTH AT HER MOORINGS—CURIOSITY OF THE PEOPLE—REFLECTIONS ON HER PROSPECTS—TIME OF HER DEPARTURE—LAST CHANCE FOR VISITORS, ETC.

" The Great Eastern steamship has once more returned to our harbour, and, as we previously predicted, the interest of the public has died out in the attractions she can supply. We have always stood up for the superiority of the Great Eastern over ordinary vessels in several respects. As a transport vessel she has no equal; as a steamboat of the first class she stands unparalleled; and as an experiment of the future results of ocean steam navigation there can be no doubt but that the ocean monster is ahead of everything else.

"The Great Eastern has had a favourable time in this country. She has cleared thousands of dollars since her arrival, and if she should remain here for a few months she will clear many thousands more. This is the great theory of the 'big ship.' But, to speak the truth, we must say that at the present moment little or no interest is exhibited in her. The excursion to Cape May, and the frightful provision made for the comfort of the passengers on that occasion, were enough to settle the prospects of the best ship of the world. We are not here making a note of the history of the vessel. Nobody has ever paid more attention to her appearance and her career since her arrival in this country than the 'Herald' has done. But we must say that the managers do not know how to 'keep a hotel.' If they did, the Cape May excursion would have been a great success, instead of a lamentable failure.

"As our readers are aware, the Great Eastern is once more in New York, and at this moment is lying off Hammond street, in the stream. Those who wish to see her had better avail themselves of their only opportunity between to-day and to-morrow. In three or four days she leaves for England, and hereafter many of our people will regret that they did not tread the deck of the greatest maritime structure that ever floated on the seas. The officers of the Great Eastern have ever conducted themselves as seamen and gentlemen, and the results of the unfortunate trip to Cape May should not be taken as a circumstance to injure their reputation. They have, as far as they are concerned, fulfilled the duty which then devolved upon them. While they remain here we hope that they will continue to be as accommodating as they have hitherto been; and if close attention and urbanity can be a recommendation to any one, then the officers of the Great Eastern are entitled to the consideration of all intelligent Americans.

"We need not describe the scenes of yesterday, as there was little to pourtray. The wharves were crowded, and, as the ship lay off in the stream she was visited by over a thousand persons. People look on this as the last view of the Great Eastern. No one expects to see her here again. We all know that there is not sufficient trade between New York and any European port to justify the employment of such an immense vessel in the carrying trade. It is, therefore, plain that those who do not now visit her will not hereafter have any opportunity of seeing her, except they cross the ocean to do so. We may mention that the Great Eastern will be open for exhibition for two days longer; and certainly there is scarcely a person who has not yet visited her that ought not to take this last opportunity of doing so. We wish the good ship well, as we always did. Forgetting all the *contretemps* of the management, and attributing them to inexperience, we sincerely hope, as do all Americans, that the good ship may once more find a safe haven in the land whence she sailed."

---

Rain continued up to midnight. Crew all day employed preparing ship for her homeward voyage. The weather cleared up early, and by four A.M. we had a fine clear morning; coaling is still going on night and day. Being our last day in New York, the ship has been better filled with visitors, although nothing like a crowd. Captain Guildford, the commander of one of Cunard's small steamers, joined to-day as our Halifax Pilot. Fine weather with a fresh northern wind. Number of visitors 6710.

*Thursday, 16th.*—This morning a writ was served against the ship for the infringement of an American patent, but upon inspection it was found " no patent at all," consequently the writ was quashed. No visitors were allowed this day. From this morning's " New York Herald ":—

"THE GREAT EASTERN.

" PREPARATIONS FOR DEPARTURE—FRESH INCREASE OF VISITORS—TEMPORARY RESUSCITATION OF BUSINESS ON THE WHARVES—THE LAST DAY OF HER VISIT—FOR ENGLAND, HO! ETC.

" There was almost a return of the old excitement yesterday on board the great mammoth ship, in consequence of the crowds that hastened to visit her ere she took her final departure from our shores. The steamers began to ply from the foot of Hammond street at ten o'clock to the vessel's station in the stream, and only ceased plying to and fro when there was no longer time left for even a cursory glance below to any whose curiosity was only to be appeased by treading her decks, if even but for a turn or two. The steamers kept up a constant communication between the vessel and shore, and on every trip they were crowded with visitors, who, having hitherto failed to visit the naval architectural wonder of the age, were at last determined that they would be able to answer affirmatively the inevitable question, ' Have you seen the Great Eastern ?'

" Notwithstanding the great numbers who went on board

during the day, and that at times there must have been at least a couple of thousand people brought together, there were but few to be encountered in any one place, so completely were they lost in the mazes of the between-decks, or engulphed in the cavernous depths below. Thus the freights of people brought over by every steamer seemed to add but little to the numbers that were already engaged in admiring the vast proportions and the extensive accommodations of the ship. As this was the last occasion that is ever likely to offer for an inspection of the mammoth of the deep, it was observable that there were more than a usual number of visitors to the engine departments, and from the manner in which the machinery and its operations were referred to and discussed, and the close scrutiny they underwent, it was clear that there was a considerable number of scientific and mechanical visitors present. There was nothing transpiring on board to indicate in the slightest degree that the great ship was spending her last day amongst us— that on the morrow those now inert and silent masses of machinery would be put into noisy motion, and that through their agency the Great Eastern, which has been so long one of the sensations of New York life, would be propelled once more to her island home across the Atlantic.

"It was supposed in the earlier days of the project, while yet the Leviathan was upon her stocks, and when, from many yards issued forth the incessant and deafening noise which proclaimed that crank and wheel and hammer and many a foundry fire was at work in speeding on the 'triumph of the age,' that Yankee vanity would be awakened, and that Yankee ingenuity would be taxed to produce a rival to the creation of his cousin John Bull. But Jonathan was content to let the work go on, wisely foreseeing that it would end in producing an ocean Frankenstein, which would be to its projectors more trouble than profit. The history of the Great Eastern has proved the wisdom of our capitalists and ship builders; and even now, when, at a fearful cost, human skill has acquired control over the great floating mass, arises the question, in the words of their own great writer, 'What will they do with it?' This is a question which comes more properly under the consideration of the Directors of the Great Ship Company, than that of a reporter, and with them let it rest.

"Yesterday the wharf at the foot of Hammond Street presented some evidences of the life and bustle which prevailed in all that neighbourhood during the palmier days of the 'wonder.' Such as the scene was yesterday, however, it would but convey a faint idea of the scenes presented and enacted ere the trip to Cape May was entered on. From the moment that the 'Herald' announced all the facts connected with that ill-managed undertaking, there was an immediate strike of tents and marquees, restaurants and confectionary saloons, segar-stands and fruit-stands, and a complete stampede of all those enterprising caterers to the public who paid anything for the privilege of doing business on the wharf. They all fled incontinently, knowing that it was in a great measure all up with the speculation. But yesterday, under the genial influence of a beautiful day succeeding a very miserable wintry one, and from the fact that this was the last day, and that a crowd of visitors would be sure to be there, the wharf was once more alive with itinerant dealers of all kinds, from the lozenge boy, with his shrill cry of 'two cents a paper,' to that great 'medicine man,' John Kemble, the original oil man, who collected an audience by the dulcet tones of an old banjo and his own voice, dreadfully cracked from his prose efforts, as he said himself. All was life and animation on the wharf; the boats went off loaded at every trip, and as they returned again fresh crowds awaited transport. The Sixth, Eighth and Ninth avenue cars were filled with the crowds hurrying to the ship, and at last, when evening came, and the boat had taken off the last loungers, it was computed that between six and seven thousand persons had been on board during the day."

The number of persons who have visited the ship during the whole time of her stay in New York, is 164,754; realising 83,296 dollars, or about £17,000. The greatest number on any one day, was on the 27th July, when there were registered, 16,817 persons; the smallest number on the 14th August, the register showing only, 1627. About 2 P.M. our passengers came on board (numbering forty-six for Halifax, and fifty-six for England). Finished coaling at 3 P.M., having received 1600 tons. We are one and all exceedingly rejoiced at leaving New York, for we have but few pleasant recollections to embitter our parting, but " unpleasant " ones crowd thick and fast on our memories. To the few kind friends, I leave behind, (who have manfully stood by officers and ship, through good and evil repute,) I beg most cordially to render the heartfelt thanks of myself and shipmates, for their many acts of kindness to us, the officers of the much-abused Great Eastern ; but I take it to be the fashion of the people here, to abuse that they cannot imitate. At 4.30 P.M. anchor up, steamed easily down the bay, commencing

## THE HOMEWARD VOYAGE.

> "The anchor's up, our sails unfurl'd,
> We're bound to plough the watery world;
> Huzza! we're Homeward Bound."

The only demonstration made in our favour afloat was by one or two mail-steamers firing a gun or two, which we answered. On shore thousands of spectators lined the wharves, to witness the departure of the "largest ship in the world," three or four ferry boats crossing the bay managed to raise a cheer; and one little yacht worked away most assiduously with a little pop-gun, till we were beyond hearing; we gave him four guns in return. Determined to behave with due politeness to the last, we eased steam off the lower battery, and saluted the American flag, with twenty-one guns, the "dipping" of the flag at the fort being the only return vouchsafed us, not one gun could they spare; however, we have the less to thank them for. At 6.25 P.M. crossed the bar, for the last time, (Cunard's steamer Australasian being close behind us, bound for Liverpool direct); stopped engines, and discharged Mr. Murphy, the pilot, (the band playing "Should auld acquaintance be forgot"); at 6.40 set on full speed for Halifax. Night fine, with light airs and hazy; at 9.30 passed Fire Island light.

*Friday, 17th August.*—Light northerly winds and fine weather. 9.30 A.M. observed the light-ship on the Nantucket shoal. At 7 P.M. stopped for a few minutes to sound in forty-eight fathoms; dark sandy bottom. The ship's speed is about fifteen knots, or seventeen miles per hour.

*Saturday, 18th.*—Light variable airs and fine weather; passed several small coasting and fishing vessels. 10 A.M. observed the land of Nova Scotia, on port-bow. P.M.—Running along the land; 2.30 observed Sambro Island right a-head; 3.40 rounded Sambro Island and entered Halifax Bay. The land about here is very rocky and barren in appearance, but improves as we proceed toward the town. When within seven miles, several small steamers, crowded with people, came to meet us, welcoming us with hearty cheers. As we drew near the town, crowds of people could be seen swarming on the wharves, vessels, and house-tops; colours were flying from ships, houses, and flag-staffs, and amidst the ringing of bells, firing of guns, and the deafening cheers of the assembled populace, the Great Eastern glided along toward her anchorage (passing within twelve feet of the vessels moored at the wharves), as completely under command as a ferry-boat. At 4.40 P.M. let go the anchor in fifteen fathoms; two royal salutes being fired on shore in honour of our arrival. We have accomplished the passage from New York, against a strong adverse current, in forty-six hours, being five-and-a-half less than the quickest on record. No sooner was our anchor at the bottom than Halifax was afloat, and the Great Eastern presented the appearance of a huge whale surrounded by a shoal of sprats; every boat and every a ology for one was brought into requisition, and "Ho! for the big ship," was the cry. After receiving " pratique," visitors were admitted on board at the charge of two shillings and sixpence. This is a very picturesque town, built on the slope of a hill, which rises in its centre, crowned with fortifications commanding the harbour, in which is a small island also well fortified. The houses are apparently well built, and streets regular, with a goodly sprinkle of churches.

The engineer's crew were all this night employed in unreefing the "floats" in the paddle wheels (before leaving Southampton these "floats" were reefed, or drawn up some five feet from the outer rings of the wheels, to lessen their immersion, and thus allow the wheels to revolve faster; they are now being "unreefed" or replaced in their original position).

*Sunday, August 19th.*—Weather cloudy with rain. 8 A.M. commenced shortening in cable (the engineer's work being completed), and at 9 our huge anchor was once more at the "cathead," and the Great Eastern steaming slowly from the harbour. An immense concourse of people was assembled on the wharves, &c., to witness our departure for "Old England"; dipped our colours, and fired four guns as a good-bye. 10 A.M. Stopped at the mouth of the bay and discharged pilot, and at 10.10 A.M. started on our voyage for Milford Haven, passing a large number of small fishing schooners. Five passengers joined us at Halifax (among them the wizard Jacobs and his brother the Goblin Sprightly,) making a total of seventy-two. Light increasing breeze from the S.E. with dull cloudy weather, and very chilly, with occasional showers, continuing the same up to midnight.

*Monday, 20th.*—Same weather. At noon we were in lat. 45° 57′ N., long. 55° 45′ W.; distance run 318 knots = 371 statute miles. Steering as we now are, nearly a due east course, we make nearly half an hour's difference of time each day, thus giving us but $23\frac{1}{2}$ hours for our day, and subtracting from the ship's run about seven miles. P.M. Moderate head winds with tolerably smooth water; middle part, thick fog. Engines going half speed for six hours, stopping four times for soundings off Cape Race. The weather towards midnight cleared up, with a light wind from the southward.

*Tuesday, 21st.*—Dull, cloudy weather, with light southerly wind.

# THE GREAT EASTERN'S LOG.

At noon we were in lat. 48° 00′ N., long. 49° 00′ W.; distance run 306 knots = 356 statute miles. Mr. Jacobs, the "Wizard, Improvisatore and Ventriloquist," (assisted by the "Goblin Sprightly,") has announced his intention to give a grand performance to-morrow evening at 8 P.M. in the first "after cargo space," where his "Theatre" is in course of erection. He intends (as he says) to "do the thing in style," as if on shore. Bills, in flaming characters, are posted in various parts of the ship, announcing that his arrival will take place in time for a performance as per hand-bill.

### GREAT EASTERN TEMPLE OF MAGIC.

NORTH ATLANTIC OCEAN,
Latitude 50° 30′ N. Longitude 38° 30′ W.

#### WEDNESDAY EVENING, AUGUST 22, 1860.

Under the immediate and distinguished Patronage of CAPT. JOHN VINE HALL, the Officers, and Passengers, of
### THE GREAT EASTERN STEAM SHIP.

The entire proceeds of the Entertainment being for the Benefit of
### THE DREADNOUGHT HOSPITAL SHIP.

### PROFESSOR JACOBS,
The world-renowned Wizard, Ventriloquist, and Improvisatore, with his inimitable
### GOBLIN SPRIGHTLY,
Having arrived at the above Latitude and Longitude have the honour to announce, for the first time in these regions, one of their
### EXTRAORDINARY PERFORMANCES!
The Wonders they introduce are unequalled in ancient or modern necromancy.
### THE SALOON,
In which this Grand Entertainment is to take place, will be fitted up as a
### TEMPLE OF ENCHANTMENT.
The Decorations in the style of Louis Quatorze. The Apparatus is of massive Silver, realising the idea of
### ALADDIN'S PALACE.

By kind permission, the Band of the Great Eastern will attend.

Commences at Eight o'clock. Admission, 4s. Back Seats, 2s. Crew, 1s.
Tickets to be obtained at the Purser's Office. No Money taken at the Doors.

Lithographs of his Temple of Magic are also to be seen in the most conspicuous places. The proceeds of this "Entertainment" (to Mr. Jacob's credit, be it said,) are to be handed to Captain Hall, and by him to the Dreadnought Hospital Ship for

Seamen of all Nations. As "all the Nobility and Gentry" in this "Great Eastern" city have promised him "their support and patronage," a "full house" is anticipated. This day has been dull and gloomy throughout, with but little wind, our noble ship making good progress through the water. Several whales came up this evening for a peep at us, as we rushed along on our way, no doubt wondering what huge monster it was thus cleaving its way through their domains. During the whole night the weather was very thick, with light, variable winds. Those mechanical contrivances of modern invention, very useful by the way, but most offensive to ears polite, ycleped steam whistles, were kept going with but little intermission, and many were the curses, both loud and deep, bestowed on them by would-be sleepers.

*Wednesday the 22nd.*—About 4 A.M. the weather cleared up a little, and by noon a light breeze sprung up from the N.W., and our forward square sails were set. The ship's position is in lat. 50° 10′ N., long. 41° 44′ W., distance run 320 knots = 363 statute miles.

The bulwarks and quarter-deck bear placards in large coloured type announcing the arrival of Professor Jacobs, and his intended performance this evening. This afternoon we passed an empty barrel floating on the water. On being asked by one of the passengers what it was, I politely informed him that it was a buoy attached to the new Atlantic Telegraph Cable ! An inoffensive sun-fish, enjoying his afternoon's siesta near the surface of the water, was capsized in a most unceremonious manner by collision with the bow of the Great Eastern: if this unfortunate denizen of the deep had any bones in its anatomical formation, doubtless they were all broken.

I do not pretend to any knowledge of the future movements of the great ship, but her present ones may be termed lively; the whole day she has been rolling about twenty-five degrees each way, proving, beyond a doubt, that she *can* roll much the same as an ordinary vessel, in the event of encountering a heavy sea. There is just now but little wind, and no sea to speak of, although it is what *we* call a cross one; however, it is pretty clearly proved that the Great Eastern (great though she be) cannot bully the waves of the Atlantic into subjection; she will have to do homage to them, the same as other vessels, by bowing and rolling, though perhaps in a less abject manner. The theatre erected for this evening's performance, presents a really creditable appearance. The space chosen is of some extent, as may be understood from the fact that it is capable of stowing over 1300 tons of cargo, its height about fourteen feet. It has been nicely carpeted, and the ship's sides hidden by flags arranged with a considerable display of artistic skill; some handsome spare chandeliers are suspended from the deck, in company with a goodly array of brightly-polished globe lamps, and a row of some fifty foot-lights, added to which some forty wax candles are burning on the stage, causing quite an illumination. In fitting up their " Temple of Magic," the Brothers Jacobs have gone to considerable trouble, in fact, as much so as if about to perform at one of the first London houses. His valuable massive silver service of " urns," " vases," " boxes," &c., his numerous and ingenious pieces of mechanism, " Liliput house," "the windmill," "blooming orange-tree," "inexhaustible bottle," &c., were all in their places; these, with the handsome stage drapery, &c., giving it the appearance (*vide* handbill) of a "Temple of Enchantment." Great credit is due to the Brothers Jacobs for the kind feeling which has prompted them at the expense of time and labour, fifty well-packed boxes having to be unpacked, and of course restored, to give this entertainment for the benefit of a public charity. The following was to be seen in various parts of the ship prior to the performance.

"NOTICE!

"Omnibuses will run, every half-hour, from 'Fore' Street, *viâ* the 'Bridges,' by which Passengers can be conveyed to Professor Jacobs' wonderful 'Temple of Magic.'

"Fare, 6*d*.

"By Order of the Honble.

"'Great Eastern' Omnibus Directors."

The performance commenced punctually at the time specified, the "house" being crowded in every part. Mr. Jacobs experienced great difficulty, from the rolling of the vessel, in keeping his apparatus in their places, many of the things fetching way and receiving considerable damage; but in spite of all these drawbacks, the Wizard for two hours delighted his audience; Goblin Sprightly keeping them in a constant state of merriment. The professor did not fail to give us a specimen of his wonderful powers as an improvvisatore. One of the subjects given him was the Great Eastern, and much amusement was afforded by the witty manner in which he handled it. The performance concluded at ten P.M., and the gratified audience departed on foot (no cabs being on the stand) for their homes in different parts of this vast city. The night was dark and cloudy, with rain. After midnight set the lower main-topsail to a strong S.W. wind, with heavy rain.

*Thursday, 23rd.*—Same weather, with a high sea running. 8 A.M. set the upper main-topsail, three trysails, and staysail; the Great Eastern, now, for the first time, having all her square sails set.

*Noon.*—Fresh S.W. winds, raining heavily, and very thick. Lat. 51° 00′ N., long. 32° 45′ W. Distance run, 340 knots = 396 statute miles. Of the numerous changes of wind and weather we are subjected to at sea, none, for discomfort, equals the weather we now have. I dare say many of my readers are familiar with the sight of a comical looking covering for the head, made of painted canvas (usually worn by coal-heavers), and generally ycleped a Sou'-Wester; so called because wet weather and S.W. winds are inseparable companions. The rain that generally accompanies this wind is not a sharp shower for an hour or so, and then giving you time to "blow," but a steady indefatigable fall, speedily finding out a sore place in a waterproof, and causing the unfortunate recipient of its bounty to feel, unlike the celebrated Mark Tapley, anything but "jolly under his difficulties." In addition to the discomfort, owing to the thick weather, which is another of the accompanying evils, there is the danger of collision, the worst, and by us, most dreaded evil of all. This wind has also brought a long, rolling sea with it; and the Great Eastern, after her yesterday's practice, has so far improved as to be now doing a most decided roll. Unsecured articles of furniture (that have stood in one position since leaving England) suddenly discover they have been wrongly placed, and the alacrity with which they place themselves anew, at some considerable distance, is rather amusing. Two of the saloon chandeliers (no doubt dissatisfied with their elevated position) sought the deck in unceremonious haste, and great was the fall thereof! Now and then, during a heavier roll than usual, a crash was heard, signalling the destruction of a few articles of crockery-ware, or a score or so of "dead marines" (empty bottles). Sundry other noises were at times heard proceeding from the bowels of the great ship, even the bulkheads (like those of ordinary vessels) condescended to creak; all tending to prove that the Great Eastern can, and doubtless will, roll when occasion offers, although due allowance must be made for the present empty state of her inside. A vocal and instrumental concert was held in the saloon this evening, and passed off with great *éclat*. Up to midnight the weather continued much the same, the wind merely veering a point or two each way, the rain continuing nearly without intermission the whole time, affording a capital opportunity of testing the efficacy of the cold water cure.

*Friday, 24th.*—Wind hauled a-head, and at 8 A.M. all square sails were furled. Still raining at intervals. At 10·15 A.M., owing to a slight derangement in some trivial portion of the machinery, the screw had to be stopped for near four hours. A screw steamer was seen on the starboard bow, but too far to the southward to make out what she was. At noon our position was in lat. 50° 58′ N., long. 24° 25′ W. Distance run, 320 knots = 373 statute miles. Soon after two P.M. our screw was again set going: by this unavoidable delay we have lost about twenty-five miles. Five trysails and a staysail are set to a moderate breeze from the northward. Weather still dull and cloudy, with occasional showers, and a cross sea running. A notice in the saloon informed all musically inclined persons, that another grand vocal and instrumental performance would be there held at eight P.M., at which time the seats were well filled, and the harmony was continued till eleven P.M., with the usual announcement of "out lights" as a *finale*. (I would mention that Mr. Jacobs entertained the company by exhibiting his wonderful powers as a ventriloquist.) The night was fine, with but little wind.

*Saturday, 25th.*—At 3.30 A.M. observed the screw-steamer Australasian on the port-bow (this is the steamer that I have mentioned as leaving New York at the same time as ourselves, bound home direct); so that taking into consideration our stay of eighteen hours in Halifax, and the détour we were compelled to make to reach that port, we have beaten her thus far twenty-four hours. Fine weather, with a light N.W. wind; square sails set forward, and others set and taken in as required.

*Noon.*—At dusk the Australasian's smoke was just visible on the port quarter; passed a barque beating to the wind, showing 1st distinguishing pendant, 183.

A lottery was formed of thirty-six members at 10s. each, to be won by the party holding the ticket with the time of the pilot's coming on board, marked on it.

The music and singing this evening was really good, and duly appreciated by the public.

> "The moon on the ocean was dimm'd by a ripple
> Affording a chequered light ;
> The gay jolly tars passed the word for the tipple
> And the toast, for 'twas 'Saturday night.'"

A private "Soirée musicale" was held in one of the officers' cabins this evening. With us 'tis

> "Always the practice, a cause of delight,
> Drinking 'sweethearts and wives' on a Saturday night."

A convivial party was assembled ; the song and joke went round, not forgetting the toast,

> "The wind that blows,
> The ship that goes,
> And the lass that loves a sailor."

A pleasant evening was spent by those who were now, perhaps, meeting for the last time, and were therefore determined it should be a merry one.

The night was fine, with light winds, fore-topsails and foresail set, although, for all their use, they might be furled. A fresh gale is required to be of any service to the Great Eastern when "running."

*Sunday 26th*, at 3.30 A.M. (daybreak). The lofty hills, and rock-bound coast of Ireland, became clearly visible, at a distance of some twelve miles.

This day we ran 346 knots = 414 statute miles. At 4 P.M. we were abreast the "Smalls," and at 4.55 stopped off the entrance to Milford Haven, and received on board a pilot. This virtually concludes our voyage, as from this up to our anchorage we several times stopped to receive on board Custom House Officials, Government Pilot, &c. The voyage from Halifax has been performed in seven days one hour (mean time).

Number of miles run by observation from New York to Milford Haven, exclusive of distance in and out of port to Pilot Stations   2980
Ditto     ditto     from Halifax   .   .   .   .   .   2357
Time between New York and Milford Haven, less 4h. 56m. difference of time   .   .   .   .   .   212h. 54m., or 13·91 knots per hour.
Time between Halifax and Milford Haven, less 3h. 15m. difference of time   .   .   .   .   .   168h. 45m., or 13·95 knots per hour.
About 16 statute miles per hour.

Steaming up to our anchorage we passed through the Channel Fleet, composed of eleven noble line of battle ships, "Old England's Wooden Walls;" from their trucks down to the decks, yards, masts, and bulwarks were crowded with "jolly tars." Each ship as we passed (her band playing "God save the Queen," or "Rule Britannia,") dipped the ensign and gave us three hearty cheers; such cheers as only British tars can give, thrilling to our hearts, and causing us to feel proud indeed of our country.

The welcome accorded to us by the British Fleet was indeed a hearty and a flattering one, one that 'twill be long 'ere we forget.

At 6.30 P.M. off Pembroke Dockyard.

" 'Stand clear the cable,' was the cry:
'The anchor's gone, we safely ride.' "

The Great Eastern has thus satisfactorily completed her first transatlantic voyage. Of her performances during that voyage, those who have read the foregoing pages may judge for themselves, whether good or bad; they will doubtless coincide with their humble servant in considering them as, in every way, most satisfactory, and that

> "She is a vessel stout and brave,
> As ever stemm'd the ocean wave."

Having (speaking in a literary sense) brought the "Great Eastern" in safety to her Haven, my task is finished, and wishing her a long and successful maritime career employed in the commerce and in the service of "Old England" (no longer as a "travelling show"), I bid adieu to the noblest structure ever raised by the hands of Englishmen.

## CONCLUSION.

Dear Reader,—Should fate, pleasure, or business, be the cause of your leaving your own fireside to visit some distant land, cast your eye over the columns of the newspapers, and if the "Great Eastern" be there advertised to sail for that port whither you are bound, take my kindly-meant advice, engage a passage in that noble vessel, and rest assured a comfortable and (as far as human foresight can provide against accidents) a safe voyage awaits you. Should you do so, we may, perchance, meet *in propriâ personâ*. If the foregoing pages have been the means of whiling away an hour or two that hung heavily on your hand, I am well repaid for my trouble, and bid you a kindly adieu.

THE "AUTHOR."

THE END.